KV-425-370

Magic's

in the

BAG

About the Authors

Jude Bradley is a writer, editor, and designer. Originally from Boston and now living in Southern California, she has worked as a journalist, TV and theater critic, and creative writing teacher. Having experienced various paranormal phenomena since the age of four, Jude now works as a spiritual consultant, using card readings, mediumship, and general energy guidance to help clients.

© www.kazphoto.com

Cheré Dastugue Coen is an award-winning journalist, instructor of writing, playwright, novelist, and cookbook author. A native of New Orleans, Cheré now makes her home in Lafayette, Louisiana, with her husband, two sons, a dog and three cats. Visit her website at www.LouisianaBookNews.com.

© Josh Coen

To Write to the Author

If you wish to contact the author or would like more information about this book, please write to the author in care of Llewellyn Worldwide and we will forward your request. Both the author and publisher appreciate hearing from you and learning of your enjoyment of this book and how it has helped you. Llewellyn Worldwide cannot guarantee that every letter written to the author can be answered, but all will be forwarded. Please write to:

Jude Bradley & Cheré Dastugue Coen
℅ Llewellyn Worldwide
2143 Wooddale Drive, Dept. 9780738719030
Woodbury, MN 55125-2989, U.S.A.

Please enclose a self-addressed stamped envelope for reply,
or $1.00 to cover costs. If outside the U.S.A., enclose
an international postal reply coupon.

Many of Llewellyn's authors have websites with additional information and resources. For more information, please visit our website at
http://www.llewellyn.com

Creating Spellbinding Gris Gris Bags & Sachets

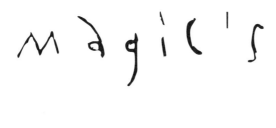

JUDE BRADLEY & CHERÉ DASTUGUE COEN

Llewellyn Publications
Woodbury, Minnesota

Magic's in the Bag: Creating Spellbinding Gris Gris Bags & Sachets © 2010 by Jude Bradley & Cheré Dastugue Coen. All rights reserved. No part of this book may be used or reproduced in any manner whatsoever, including Internet usage, without written permission from Llewellyn Publications, except in the case of brief quotations embodied in critical articles and reviews.

First Edition
First Printing, 2010

Book design by Steffani Sawyer
Cover design by Kevin R. Brown
Cover images: Black Bag © iStockphoto.com/Kirn
               Coin © iStockphoto.com/Živa Duncan Walker
               Figure and Star © Image Club
               Rabbit's foot, Leaf, Cinnamon sticks and Rock © PhotoDisc
Interior photos © Cheré Dastugue Coen

Llewellyn is a registered trademark of Llewellyn Worldwide Ltd.

Library of Congress Cataloging-in-Publication Data
Bradley, Jude, 1958–
  Magic's in the bag : creating spellbinding gris gris bags & sachets /
Jude Bradley & Cheré Dastugue Coen.—1st ed.
      p. cm.
  Includes bibliographical references and index.
  ISBN 978-0-7387-1903-0 (alk. paper)
  1. Magic—Louisiana—New Orleans. 2. Voodooism—Louisiana—New
Orleans. 3. New Orleans (La.)—Religious life and customs. I. Coen,
Cheré Dastugue. II. Title. III. Title: Magic's in the bag.
  BF1621.B68 2010
  133.4'4—dc22
                  2010035349

Llewellyn Worldwide does not participate in, endorse, or have any authority or responsibility concerning private business transactions between our authors and the public.

All mail addressed to the author is forwarded but the publisher cannot, unless specifically instructed by the author, give out an address or phone number.

Any Internet references contained in this work are current at publication time, but the publisher cannot guarantee that a specific location will continue to be maintained. Please refer to the publisher's website for links to authors' websites and other sources.

Note: The authors and publisher of this book are not responsible in any manner whatsoever for any injury that may occur through following the instructions or advice contained herein. The recipes and remedies in this book are not meant to diagnose, treat, prescribe, or substitute for consultation with a licensed health-care professional. New herbal substances should always be used in small amounts to allow the body to adjust and to test for possible allergic reactions.

Llewellyn Publications
A Division of Llewellyn Worldwide Ltd.
2143 Wooddale Drive
Woodbury, Minnesota 55125
www.llewellyn.com

Printed in the United States of America

To Bruce, Josh, and the two Taylors—
They that light our lives and keep us sane while driving us crazy.

Contents

Author Introductions

By Jude Bradley

When my grandfather died in 1962, my mother's unmarried sister moved in with us. Alyce, a striking woman with large eyes and a pure heart, was my mother's oldest sister. Private by nature, she was thrifty, but also unceasingly generous and indefinably wise. She took charge of the grounds of our house almost immediately. We had a large yard, with rich black soil that could grow a Buick from a spare tire. Alyce loved to work the soil, feel it between her fingers and roll it around in her hands. When she worked in the yard, her face would take on an indescribable serenity.

Alyce planted dozens of marigolds around the perimeter of our house and lilac bushes here and there. Rambling roses, bright pink and pungent, climbed along the fences and a healthy grapevine wound through a thick white trellis beside the driveway. Crocuses sprouted like clockwork every spring, their emerging faces symbols of punctuality and renewal. And a tiny pine tree guarded the end of the dirt driveway. I was small, but could touch the top with my finger when she lifted me up.

When we traveled, Alyce collected pinecones and kept them in her apartment at the back of our house. She saved dried flowers, filling bowl after bowl with their purples, pinks, and reds, and she gathered the peeling white bark of birch trees to place in small dishes near candles.

Shells were also a big part of her life. Twice every summer, we would venture to the beaches of Cape Cod and Alyce would gather shells with ritualistic passion. She chose carefully, filling buckets with shell pieces and occasionally whole shells. Once in a while, a dried horseshoe crab would become part of the décor. At home, she had bottles and jars filled with the ocean memories. (When I shake the bottles now, the rattle of the shells reminds me of the sounds of the waves tumbling toward the shoreline.)

Stones adorned both my mother's part of the house and Alyce's. There were bits of white quartz on windowsills and end tables, set high in corners, and displayed on bookshelves. Each had been carefully selected for its color, but usually the stones' energy was what would attract both Mom and Alyce. When I'd ask either of them what the stones meant, the answer was always the same: luck.

Whether or not the stones provided them with luck remains a question. At times, things were definitely tough, but we never wanted for anything, we were all healthy, and my father always had a job. Although we never fell into big money, my mother had a special talent for regularly winning the smaller jackpots in the state lottery. It occurred to me over time that my mother and aunt's wishes were simple, founded in a Depression mentality—sustenance was paramount, and an unfettered sense of security was nearly all one could ask from the universe.

Alyce was the first to go of the "old group." My mother's other sister, Lily, followed next, and my mother was the last. Lily, who lived in the neighboring town with her family, was much like her sisters, a great lover of nature. Her perfect house was set far from the street and surrounded by enormous maple and ash trees. She was adept in canning and, like my mother and Alyce, saved bits of the Earth for her own personal reasons.

Upon Alyce's passing, I was left with many questions as I realized that there was more to her collecting and gardening habits than I'd originally thought. I slowly realized how steeped in superstition her habits had been. She believed in bits of magic, and surrounded herself throughout her life with tiny assurances and reminders that she would always be connected to nature. I learned much from her over the years, but even more after she'd left this plane.

It became part of my nature as well to collect stones, shells, and dried plants that spoke to me in one way or another. Even years later, I feel Alyce with me all of the time. I hear the whisper of her gentle voice behind me every day. She reminds me of who I am—that I am a part of my long past, my ancestors, as well as a part of the future. Now, when I look at my teenage daughter, I realize the importance of infusing this same spirit in her.

When I was a child, I didn't know that the marigolds surrounding our house were for protection; the crocuses and rose bushes infusions of love; and the pine tree for healing, protection, and money. The grapevine embodied garden magic and wealth, and the strategically planted lilacs protected our home from malevolent spirits. Every part of the natural world that Alyce and my mother gathered had a meaning far beyond its beauty—with their plants and stones, they created a safe haven for children to grow and prosper. They practiced their beliefs in private, but with a public display of color and magic.

When I met my friend and colleague Cheré Coen, I knew that I had found a kindred spirit. We discussed our histories, our families, and our dreams, quickly coming to the conclusion that our paths had likely crossed in previous lives. An inherent thread connected us, and we are sure that the undeniable magic of the universe brought us together to work on this book.

Although our experiences were in some ways vastly different, divided as they were by geography and tradition, we are bound by our unyielding beliefs. We believe that our collective knowledge of Earth magic can speak to many people. I have been blending herbs for most of my adult life, as well as practicing the solitary craft and working part-time as a psychic and medium. Creative writing and journalism were what brought Cheré and me together, and those same skills guided us in the writing of *Magic's in the Bag*. We share a love for the craft as well as a love for the written word. As we weave our symbiotic thread into the pages that follow, we hope you can also hear the voices of our ancestors as they guide us toward a higher spiritual plane.

By Cheré Dastugue Coen

When I tell people in South Louisiana that I'm working on a book about gris gris, eyebrows raise. When someone mentions gris gris today, it's generally not in a positive way. For instance, "I'm going to put some gris gris on you" means someone's about to throw some bad luck your way (although it's rare for South Louisianans to really mean it—we love to joke).

Still, somewhere along the way, American culture has associated gris gris with bad spells and negative conjuring. But this is more aligned with Hollywood than with reality. We've forgotten those wonderful stories of our ancestors dusting secret herbal powders into the corners of the house for protection and enlisting saints and spirits for assistance. We've also forgotten the longstanding tradition of the gris gris bag—with its lucky herbs, bones, and stones that can help us find a job or win the lottery (to name just a few uses).

I met Jude Bradley in Southern California when we were both working at a Hollywood entertainment trade publication. Neither of us was happy in our positions, so I created a gris gris bag especially for Jude to help her find new employment. She was thrilled with the creation (the fact that she loves exotic things from New Orleans might have had something to do with it!), but she kept insisting that I write a book about gris gris and show others how to create their own bags. A few years later, Jude had moved on to new work, but signs kept pointing me in this direction. Again, Jude insisted that I needed to write a book. I finally agreed—but only if Jude wrote it with me.

And so here we are. As journalists, we are addicted to research, and have painstakingly investigated the history of magical bags throughout the ages. But ultimately, I view gris gris–making as something natural, something that's second nature. I grew up in New Orleans, where you can still find gris gris bags sitting on a store counter with names like *Lover Come to Me* or *Lotto Help*. As a medium, card reader, and house blesser, Jude brings her own unique attributes to the project. She creates bags that speak of her Wiccan tradition and her home state of Massachusetts.

Together, our bags rock.

But don't just take our word for it. We've had lots of positive feedback from those who've received our bags. For example, a writer friend of ours was struggling to make a living, so I sent her a green gris gris bag full of prosperity herbs. Not long afterwards, she won a three-book contract. She said it was a combination of luck and hard work—and although she could handle the hard work part, luck was something she'd wanted some help with. Enter the gris gris bag.

Another writer friend, Christee Atwood, has said that her bag was "nothing short of miraculous." She received her gris gris—her "wonderful talisman," as she calls it—right before she sold her first book, and has kept it in a place of honor through the writing of five more books, noting that "it's been more valuable to my writing career than that college writing class I took in '79." And when my Canadian (and distant Cajun) cousin, Susanne MacDonald, lost her job, I mailed her an employment gris gris bag. She reported that "within a couple of weeks" of receiving the bag, she got a job at a radio station.

You may still be asking yourself, does gris gris work? Are these examples just lucky coincidences? Well, first of all, you have to believe—as my mother, a motivational speaker, would say. Create your bag in light of your wishes, then put it in a place where you can see and smell it every day; this will remind you of your desires and of the energy heading in your direction. Also, be sure to look at the discussion in this book about the history of humankind's relationship to nature's gifts. How can we doubt the influence of king basil, or the guidance of quartz crystals, when cultures worldwide have enlisted their aid for centuries?

Above all, remember this: a gris gris bag is part of nature—just like you are—and nature in all its glory can bring us anything we desire.

Bon chance!

part one

Overview

THE MAGIC THROUGH THE AGES
. . . .

A tribe of men and women scurry about the unspoiled Earth, wrestling with their basic instincts, not quite thinking beings, yet no longer animals. They gaze up at the full moon, its bright perfection lighting the night as they gather tools for the morning hunt. Fashioned from nature and mimicking nature, they join in ceremony near the stone walls where they make their homes. A single hand lifts a chunk of charred wood, thick with pitch from the dying fire, and marks upon the wall. Images of their hunt. They can see it well before its advent.

A Shaman in the Desert

Some theorists speculate that cave drawings were the earliest form of positive visualization. In these first human societies, people clustered together for survival. They hunted animals and gathered berries and nuts that grew wild around them. Social structures were beginning to form: parents loved their children, and the tribe honored its elders. Spirituality was also in its onset, as people began to perceive the larger cosmic forces around them. The idea of writing was eons away, so the story of the hunt was told through pictographs. Drawings also showed where there were trees bearing seeds and fruit, and how to find the way to water.

In 2006, a group of archaeologists unearthed a remarkable discovery near modern-day Jerusalem: an ancient tribe of early humans, believed to be part of the Natufian culture, was not merely hunting and gathering but living within a rudimentary society. As a

Mesolithic culture, the Natufians existed in pre-agricultural times, but the archaeological digs revealed an unexpected level of settled civilization among this peaceful, non-nomadic Natufian tribe.

Most significantly, excavators uncovered the much-honored grave of a small woman, buried deep within the dry, unforgiving earth. She had been deformed since birth, twisted into something not quite right by the hand of a greater being, and it was apparent that the tribe revered her. What her deformities took away from her in terms of her life, her people made up for with honor. This woman was considered the gifted one—she was blessed by magic and connected to the Earth, and cared for within their tiny world.

Carefully placed within the gravesite and around her huddled body were various bones, a cow tail, an eagle wing, the foot of another human being, and as many as fifty tortoise shells. Archaeologists found the complete forearm of a wild boar beneath the woman's arm, which is a strong suggestion that her people attributed a type of animist power to her. This woman was a shaman to her tribe—most likely a healer, a magician, a wise woman, and perhaps a clairvoyant.

The discovery of the tribe and its shaman opened the door to a world that existed twelve to fifteen thousand years ago. Serious doubt had now been cast on the view that life at this point in prehistory was simple. The Natufian tribe had formed a settlement, the family was a recognized unit, and spiritual beliefs had apparently found their way into the hearts and minds of the people. Their life was about more than survival.[1]

During the Neolithic (or "New Stone Age") period, humankind at large moved away from hunting and gathering as agricultural practices became more widespread. People in many societies began using bits of nature to aid them in their spiritual needs as well as in their practical ones.

---

1. "Skeleton of 12,000-Year-Old Shaman Discovered Buried with Leopard, 50 Tortoises and Human Foot." ScienceDaily.com (accessed September 2010).

It is impossible, of course, to pinpoint when the idea of the soul first came into being. Evidence appears sporadically much earlier than was commonly thought, as with the Natufians' elaborate burial of the shamanic woman. The homage at this burial site clearly indicates the tribe's belief that death was not the final curtain, but just a precursor to another existence.

At the same time as the Natufians, but thousands of miles away, Native American cultures that valued spiritual objects were beginning to emerge. Nomadic tribes carried items with them on their travels, such as bones and shells indigenous to their region. These items were even more precious to the tribes for whom they were unfamiliar, and were so valued that they were worn as adornments, sewn into clothing, braided into hair, or carried in pouches. These pouches of tools, medicinal plants, and items for trade, which were worn around the neck or waist, became cross-cultural among tribes and were used for both spiritual and practical purposes. Likewise, tribes learned the medicinal properties of plants, and recognized the many helpful uses of trees and stones, for both religious and pragmatic reasons. Native American spiritual practices evolved around the core idea of the natural world—honoring the Earth was paramount.

Amulets & Charms

The plants, stones, and precious objects that such cultures revered—and often carried in bags—became in essence amulets and charms. While the presence of amulets and charms was commonplace across cultures, the difference between the two seems to depend on the particular belief system of the culture. At the most basic level, an amulet is "a device, the purpose of which is to protect, but by magical and not physical means." For instance, "a lump of meteorite worn against gunpowder is an amulet, a bullet-proof vest is not." Meanwhile, "a charm is something to bring good luck, health and happiness. In so doing it might also be expected to protect from bad luck, sickness and misery..."[2]

Another way to think of the difference between an amulet and a charm is that an amulet is "any object which by its contact or its close proximity to the person who owns it, or to any possession of his, exerts power for his good, either by keeping evil from him and his property, or by endowing him with positive advantages."[3] It is "a charm (as an ornament) often inscribed with a magic incantation or symbol to aid the wearer or protect against evil (as disease or witchcraft)."[4]

The Kikuyu of Africa, for instance, protected themselves by placing powders inside an assortment of cloths blessed by a medicine man and carrying it with them. In other parts of Africa, and in central Asia, plants and herbs and sometimes desires written on paper were bundled within a leather bag or swaths of fabric. On the Greek island of Karpathos, which is said to have been settled as early as the Neolithic period, triangular pieces of cloth were stuffed with secret ingredients and decorated with beads to protect a person while traveling.

In Egypt, amulets were carried for protection and to enlist the assistance of the gods, then were buried with the departed in tombs for guidance in the afterlife. These elaborate burials clearly demonstrate the ancient Egyptians' extreme commitment to spirituality. Before death, individuals paid fortunes to spiritual scribes to construct "personalized" guides to help them make the journey to the other side; the template for these guides is what is now known as *The Book of the Dead*. The ancient Egyptians called this text "Spells of Emerging in Daytime"; it was replete with spells, incantations, and detailed instructions regarding what elements from the Earth should be gathered together to assure the deceased a safe passage to the afterlife.

---

2. Sheila Paine, *Amulets: Sacred Charms of Power and* Protection (Rochester, VT: Inner Traditions, 2004).

3. Campbell Bonner, *Studies in Magical Amulets* (Ann Arbor, MI: University of Michigan Press, 1950).

4. *Merriam-Webster's Collegiate Dictionary, 11th Edition* (2003).

While the precise origin of spell sachets, medicine bags, and pouches is as difficult to pinpoint as the origins of society itself, it is significant that the practice of gathering and valuing sacred objects from the Earth transcends all geographic and cultural boundaries.

Gris Gris, Mojos, & More

In the American South, there's an old tradition among African-Americans of collecting ingredients—usually "sticks, stones, roots, and bones"[5]—and placing them inside a flannel cloth, preferably red, as a magical amulet. These "gris gris" or "mojo" bags are used for things like luck in gambling, attracting love, stopping gossip, and warding off evil. Other names for this traveling bag of magic include mojo hand, conjure bag, juju, trick bag, nation sack, root bag, toby, jomo, and lucky hand (referring to the lucky hand root, one of the more common ingredients used inside a gris gris bag). The origin of the word "gris gris" is unclear, but consensus points to the Central African word *gri-gri* or *gree-gree*, which means "fetish" or "charm." The word "mojo" is derived from the West African *mojuba*, meaning "prayer."

Most people associate gris gris with hoodoo, voodoo, or the voudon religion. What is practiced with a gris gris bag is essentially a combination of voudon (a West African religion where priests and sorcerers used herbs and magic for folk healing and hexing) and North American influences. Slaves from West Africa brought their traditions and beliefs into Haiti, and that system of voodoo arrived in America, most predominantly through New Orleans. What many people practice in New Orleans today is actually a combination of Catholicism, voodoo, and the old African beliefs.

Richard Persico, a social anthropologist at Georgia Southern University, claims that Africa's Yoruba gods took on the identities of saints in Catholic areas. In addition, Native Americans influenced

---

5. Stephanie Rose Bird, *Sticks, Stones, Roots* & Bones (Woodbury, MN: Llewellyn Publications, 2004).

the practice.[6] Due to the lack of certain plants in the new North American environment, hoodoo/voodoo practitioners had to "adopt Native American and even European plant allies and practices in their work," resulting in "the fusion of many plant magic strands," as authors Heaven and Charing explain.[7] Persico points out that "Religion, magic, and healing were all part of the same package"—in sum, "what they all have in common is the notion that supernatural power can be invested in things."[8]

Some historians claim that the voudon practice of spell or gris gris bags originated in an enslaved society's desire to have power over their lives. If slaves believed they would be protected from a beating by putting a hex, or a gris gris, on the master, the bag gained enormous power. "There is much superstition among the slaves," Henry Bibb wrote in 1849, in his memoirs *Narrative of the Life and Adventures of Henry Bibb, An American Slave, Written by Himself.* "Many of them believe in what they call 'conjuration,' tricking, and witchcraft; and some of them pretend to understand the art, and say that by it they can prevent their masters from exercising their will over their slaves. Some are often applied to by others, to give them power to prevent their masters from flogging them."

The Power of Intent

Persico interviewed root doctors in rural Georgia and found that if people believe a gris gris has been put upon them (say, a spell to cause them to become ill), their mind may enact that scenario and the person will actually become sick. One compelling example of this kind of force at work was reported in 2004 by *The Advocate* newspaper in Baton Rouge. Members of the Bayou Vermilion District Watershed often find small prescription bottles washed up on

---

6. Quoted in Don Schanche, Jr. "Ancient Beliefs Still Alive in Georgia" (*The Macon Telegraph*, circa 2000).

7. *Plant Spirit Shamanism: Traditional Technique for Healing the Soul* (Rochester, VT: Destiny Books, 2006).

8. Schanche, op. cit.

the shores of the Vermilion River, each containing a slip of paper with writing on it, colored powder, and occasionally cayenne and other herbs. The notes ask for spells to be extinguished or granted. Of course, the people who write these requests believe in the magic—and apparently, so did one of the workers who pulled them out. She became ill upon reading the words.

But this connection between the human mind and real-life events can work in a positive direction as well. Gris gris bags are, in essence, a prayer or magical spell you can carry around with you to serve as a reminder of your intention. Author Ray T. Malbrough offers a helpful explanation of how belief can shape reality, describing a gris gris bag as "a psycho-spiritual support; it implies faith." Like any amulet, the bag

> serves to intensify the faith in yourself that through the help of the gris-gris bag you will obtain this or receive that. In order to strengthen your faith in the effectiveness of the gris-gris bag, there must be a complete understanding of what each item you put into your gris-gris bag symbolizes. This is important because the items used act as a psychological aid to strengthen the link between the desire and the mind of the individual whose energy will be used in making the gris-gris bag.[9]

Malbrough adds that thoughts produce force and energy, and thinking of one's desire will make it happen: "In making a gris gris bag, a certain thought pattern is created and set into motion."[10] This is a simple application of the much-touted "law of attraction"—the basic belief that "what the mind can conceive and believe, it can achieve," as Napoleon Hill put it. This is easier said than done, of

---

9. *Charms, Spells and Formulas* (Woodbury, MN: Llewellyn, 2002).

10. Ibid.

course, and one point made by reputable "law of attraction" books is the importance of specificity of intent. In *Think and Grow Rich* (1937), Hill devoted an entire chapter to "Organized Planning," where he encouraged readers to have a painstakingly specific plan of action. Likewise, when creating a gris gris, knowing exactly what you're trying to achieve, and creating the conditions for its manifestation, is as vital an element for success as belief in success.

In *Spirit Healing: How to Make Your Life Work*, Mary Dean Atwood explains the same phenomenon in energetic terms. "If you think with emotion," she writes, "thought particles form faster and travel greater distances." Accordingly, "the more emotion in your thought or wish, the more likely it is to materialize. … Peaceful or beautiful wishes and thoughts must be accompanied by sincerity and love to speed them on their way toward formation." She points out that Native American priests and shamans knew of the power of intention and asked their spiritual guides for assistance, "knowing that their prayers would be heard and hoping that their requests would be honored. Intensity of emotion and sincerity was always present, along with self-sacrifice and honor."

Gris Gris Ingredients

Herbs known for their magical properties, the bones and teeth of deceased animals, sticks, stones (precious and otherwise), and roots such as High John the Conqueror can all be used in a modern gris gris bag. Lucky charms, four-leaf clovers, silver dimes, personal objects, and other items that resonate with the maker of the bag can be included as well. The more intimately personal the object added—such as hair and fingernail clippings—the greater the bag's effectiveness.

The ingredients placed in each bag are selected based on the intention behind the bag. For example, a gris gris to attract money, called a "prosperity bag," might include black-eyed peas, nutmeg, mojo beans, and five-finger grass, along with a silver coin and a rabbit's foot. As you place these items (and perhaps a personal object) inside a green bag, visualize the arrival of prosperity by the light of a green candle.

Your gris gris is now complete.

Gather your ingredients and candles when you're ready to assemble your bag.

Traditionally, gris gris spells concluded with the sprinkling of some type of liquid to "fix" the mojo—this could be anything from whiskey to specially made oils with names like "Lover Come to Me" or "Neighbor Be Gone." Heaven and Charing write that the bag "is purified in incense and its spirit 'fed' with rum or whiskey and with Florida Water." They note that "body fluids may also be used, especially if the charm is to influence another person." If a man wishes to encourage a woman to fall in love with him, for instance, he might dab "a little of her sweat, urine, or saliva" on the bag (and placing the desired lover's hair or nail clippings within the bag helps, too).[11]

In our work, we focus our power on the ingredients assembled, the visualization involved, and the power of thought and intent—resulting in the creation of a bag that most represents our desires. In this book, accordingly, we emphasize the basic creation of a bag and leave the choice of whether to add that final "fixing" up to you. Also, we adamantly insist that bones and other parts of animals only

11. *Plant Spirit Shamanism*, op cit.

be included if they are found naturally fallen in the wild or are the remnants of a meal, such as chicken bones. No animal should ever be harmed in the making of a gris gris bag.

Black Magic

What gris gris bags and spell sachets *must not* be associated with is black magic (magic conducted with the assistance of evil energies or with evil intent). Remember that any power sent into the universe falls back upon its wisher, and spells cast upon people to do them harm will only injure the conjurer. And, although there are many who believe in sensationalized myths about voodoo practices (which are reinforced by the unfortunate proliferation of Chinese-made voodoo dolls and other souvenirs in New Orleans gift shops), voodoo priests and priestesses hold that "black magic" per se does not exist for them. In fact, the authors of *Voodoo, Secret Power in Africa* report that "the most eminent voodoo priest in Benin, Sossa Guedehoungue, maintains that black magic is in contradiction to voodoo, and that anyone who has another person bewitched is arrogating divine powers to themselves." From the voodoo perspective, "it is for the gods to decide whether and how a person should be punished for a transgression."[12]

It is important to recognize, as you build your gris gris, that the power of positive energy is the greatest power in the universe. Taking a constructive approach when making your bag will prove far more beneficial than coming from a place of anger or revenge. Even if your intention originates in a negative situation, be sure to alter your perspective before gathering your ingredients—and enjoy the positive results.

Our Version of Gris Gris & Spell Sachets

The advice, instructions, and spells you will find in this book are based on the long history of gris gris and mojo bags, Native American lore concerning medicine pouches, Wiccan spell sachets, and

---

12. Henning Christoph and Hans Oberlander, *Voodoo, Secret Power in Africa* (Cologne, Germany: Taschen, 1996).

ancient Greek, Roman, Egyptian, and Celtic understandings of how items from nature can be used to bring specific intentions to fruition. The lists of the magical properties of plants and stones are based on historical records, as well as on legends and mythology that date back to ancient times. As authors, we do not claim to be representative of any one religion, nor are we specifically following the practices of the voudon faith. For simplicity's sake, we decided to refer to our creations simply as "gris gris bags" and "spell sachets," and for spells that call for sweet or prophetic dreams, we call the bags "pillow sachets" or "dream pillows."

In addition, we don't insist on there being only one way to create a spell bag, but rather provide guidelines that have been used over the centuries. Remember that none of these guidelines is set in stone. Individual tastes, particularly when a bag is created for your own use, should be embraced and utilized. You must let your own energies guide you. Since you will be the one enjoying the bag, make the experience personal and heartfelt. Also, feel free to decorate your bag using decorative fabrics and beads, charms, or other items.

If you create a gris gris bag for another person, visualizing good thoughts of that person while assembling the bag always produces good results. Chanting positive affirmations or saying prayers for the person's health and happiness works well too. Once the bag is given, however, the recipient must make it his or her own. We recommend that the recipient place a personal item, such as a fingernail clipping or hair, inside the bag, then light a candle and ask the bag for assistance. From that moment on, the spell bag will belong fully to the person who has received it.

PUTTING IT ALL TOGETHER
· · · · · · · · · · · · · · · ·

There are several things to consider as you prepare to create your gris gris bag. The phase of the moon, the day of the week, the color of the bag, and what items will be placed inside should all correspond with your intention for the bag. If, for instance, you discover that the time (moon phase or day) isn't right for assembling a specific kind of bag, make a plan. Let's say you want to attract wealth, but it's a weekend and the moon is waning. It's best to wait until the moon turns to waxing and initiate your charm on a Thursday.

Your state of mind is also very important. Creators of gris gris bags must focus all their power, with love and optimism, on their intention, whether the bag is for themselves or for someone else. An effective gris gris bag is based in constructive visualization and constant faith in its intention. So it is important to clearly know what your intention is before you even start to collect ingredients or sew the bag. Be as specific as possible, then think about what elements around you spark that intention within you. Follow your instincts.

The assembly of the bag—putting the items within it and concentrating on your intention—is a form of ritual. It is interesting that a significant aspect of making intention "work" is the combination of faith and ritual. Of course, the idea of ritual can be at once frightening and intriguing, since rituals are often shrouded in mystery by secret societies committed to keeping them private, or replete with motions, chants, incense, incantations, and prayer. Given such shared elements, it becomes apparent that the rituals of the Christian church are not so different from those performed in a synagogue, a mosque, a temple, or under the open sky. And the reason for all the pomp, whatever the context of the ritual, is the need for emotional connectivity. Rituals invariably enhance focus—they create an energy partnership between the soul and the greater surroundings.

The Power of Seven in the Bag

One of the first questions you will face while selecting objects for your bag is how many (or how few) you will put within it. Any number of items can be included in a gris gris—*as long as the combination adds up to an odd number,* and as long as there are at least three ingredients and no more than thirteen. Keep in mind that if you add your own elements (such as a fingernail clipping or lock of hair), the final count in the bag still needs to be an odd number. Also keep this in mind if you're making the bag as a gift. Since the recipient should add something of themselves to the bag, you would contribute an even number and instruct the recipient to add an element, bringing the final number of items to an odd number.

For simplicity and continuity's sake, we advocate seven items per bag. Note that the number seven also corresponds to the days of the week, the moon phases used in spell bag creation, and crystalline structures. Plus, the seven chakras in the human body correlate with the colors red, orange, yellow, green, blue, indigo, and violet. These are the basic colors for gris gris spells, illustrating the electromagnetic power of color and its relationship to both our bodies and psyches.

As you form your intention, be sure to recognize the incredible power of the self (the one) and the influence you have over the six directions that radiate from you. Keep in mind the symbol of the cube—with its six surfaces and mysterious seventh point within—as you form your intention. The six surfaces represent the directions: north, east, south, west, up, and down. In the middle is the one point from which radiate six pyramids. Given the power of this seventh point, the "heptad"—the number seven—has long been viewed as sacred; ancient cultures called it "worthy of veneration."[13] For medieval scholars, the number seven represented the union between the four elements of the material world and the three "holy" or spiritual realms of heaven, earth, and underworld. The ancient Egyptians considered seven symbolic of eternal life and of a complete cycle; it simultaneously embodies "bringing all things

---

13. Manly P. Hall, *The Secret Teachings of All Ages* (New York: Jeremy P. Tarcher/Penguin, 2003).

into existence as well as change."[14] It marks both "the beginning and the ending of a cycle—'alpha and omega.'"[15]

Seven figures predominately in religion: according to Genesis, God created the world in six days and rested on the seventh. There are seven deadly sins, seven virtues, and seven archangels, plus numerous references to seven in the Jewish faith. The Unitarian-Universalists abide by seven principles. And here are just a few more reasons to like seven: there are seven continents and seven seas, seven ages of man, seven wonders of the world, Rome had seven emperors and seven hills, seven notes make up the musical scale, there are seven colors in the color spectrum, and of course, Snow White befriended seven dwarfs.

"What about the seven-point rating scale, the seven categories for absolute judgment, the seven objects in the span of attention, and the seven digits in the span of immediate memory?" cognitive psychologist George A. Miller wrote in 1956. "For the present I propose to withhold judgment. Perhaps there is something deep and profound behind all these sevens, something just calling out for us to discover it. But I suspect that it is only a pernicious, Pythagorean coincidence."[16] In sum, regardless of the many reasons to focus on the number seven (or not), it apparently is the perfect number for the human brain to remember and use.

You could argue that five is a better number for luck, as it's the "holy protector" of casinos, or that three symbolizes birth, life, and death. Nine represents three times three, and thus is a triad of triads; plus, there were nine sacred herbs. Nine is also the symbolic number of completion—therefore, nine items in your gris gris bag may prove effective if your intention involves finishing a daunting task. A little research can suggest which number best suits your specific needs.

---

14. Sandra Kynes, *Your Altar: Creating a Sacred Space for Prayer and Meditation*.

15. G.A. Gaskell, *Dictionary of All Scriptures and Myths* (New York: Avenel Books, 1960).

16. George A. Miller, "The Magical Number Seven, Plus or Minus Two: Some Limits on Our Capacity for Processing Information" (*The Psychological Review* 63, 1956).

All told, there are many good numbers, depending on your intention. And we leave your intention up to you.

Phases of the Moon

An awareness of the phase of the moon is important in making gris gris bags, because it can strengthen or otherwise affect your intention, and therefore the power of the bag itself.

Waxing Moon

The two-week phase when the moon grows in the sky, from the darkness of the new moon to its full size as a full moon, is called the waxing of the moon. During this time, create gris gris bags with spells for attraction, growth, prosperity and gain, increase of health, forming relationships, and developing creative projects.

Full Moon

When the moon is full, the pull of the moon's energy is at its highest. Utilize this strong lunar energy by making gris gris bags for love, creativity, healing, fertility, prosperity, goals, and success.

Waning Moon

After the full moon, the moon begins its two-week waning phase, diminishing from its full size to a half, then a quarter, and finally to a darkened stage. This waning period is a good time to create gris gris bags for eliminating problems, overcoming obstacles and problems, or removing curses or negativity. Starting a weight-loss program or trying to break a habit is more effective when the accompanying spells occur during this period.

Dark Moon

When the moon moves directly between the Earth and sun, so that its illuminated side is fully facing the sun, it wanes to darkness from the perspective of the Earth. This is called a dark moon, and the phase lasts from one to three days.

During a dark moon, lunar energy is at its lowest. This is a great time for reflection and rest. Creating gris gris bags should be avoided during this time.

New Moon

When the moon and sun are still in conjunction but the waxing energy of the next cycle has begun, it is called (astronomically speaking) the new moon. As with a dark moon, the moon is invisible in the sky, but its energy has begun to increase as it grows toward a crescent. It will strengthen within the following two weeks as it grows into a full moon.

During the new moon, create gris gris bags for new beginnings such as a new job, new love, new venture, new creative endeavor, etc.

Blue Moon

The moon's cycle in relation to the Earth occurs every twenty-nine and a half days. Because almost all of the months have more days than the moon's cycle, two full moons will occur within a month's time about every two and a half years. This extra full moon in a calendar month is called a "blue moon."

Because it's considered rare to see two full moons within one month, the blue moon spawned an expression "once in a blue moon" to mean something happening infrequently. Although blue moons in general really aren't that rare, having two blue moons occur within a year's time *is* rare. In 2018, blue moons will visit both January and March.

Because a blue moon is both a full moon with strong energy and a semi-rare occurrence, take this time to review your past and learn what worked and didn't work. This is much like thinking through resolutions on New Year's Eve, and is a good time to set new goals and activate them through the appropriate gris gris bag. Many Wiccans and Pagans call the blue moon a "goal moon" for this reason. It's a great chance for new beginnings.

Days of the Week

The days of the week can likewise establish a meaning and energy around your bag. The list below outlines some of the basic elements to be aware of.

Sunday

Bag color: Yellow or gold
Astrological influence: Sun
Mineral: Gold
Spells: Healing and health, good fortune, peace and harmony or preventing conflict, recovering lost property

Monday

Bag color: Silver or white
Astrological influence: Moon
Mineral: Silver
Spells: Dreams, family, home and hearth, childbirth/female fertility, medicine, creativity

Tuesday

Bag color: Red or orange
Astrological influence: Mars
Mineral: Iron
Spells: Courage, sexual energy, passion, overthrowing enemies

Wednesday

Bag color: Purple or blue
Astrological influence: Mercury
Mineral: Mercury
Spells: Communications, travel, knowledge (Blue bag only: healing and health)

Thursday

Bag color: Green
Astrological influence: Jupiter
Mineral: Tin

Spells: Wealth, good luck, business expansion and/or success, career, legal matters, ambition, desires

Friday
Bag color: Pink
Astrological influence: Venus
Mineral: Copper
Spells: Romantic love, friendship, beauty, the arts, social activities

Saturday
Bag color: White or black
Astrological influence: Saturn
Mineral: Lead
Spells: Protection, life's pathway, resolution (white bag) and psychic self-defense, protection from evil (black bag)

Colors

Choosing colors and how to display them with your bag is one of the most enjoyable aspects of creating a gris gris bag. Consider the nuances of colors thoughtfully when selecting your materials.

Black

Black is probably the color with the most characteristics. Wall Street bankers and lawyers traditionally wear black suits, and women wear black dresses and men wear black tuxes to elegant gatherings. The color black also provokes feelings of melancholy, thus the expression "black mood." Black is the predominant color for funerals in the Western world. And a "black sheep" is someone who doesn't fit in—not exactly a positive connotation for the color.

But black can also serve as a powerful protection color. Keep in mind that, within the color spectrum, white is the combination of all colors and black is the absence of color. As a strong representative of the absence of influence, black can serve to represent a non-zone: a place where negative effects are eliminated.

Black is also a major force color in the mystical world. Given all its negative connotations, black is necessarily contrasted with white, as in the yin/yang symbol. It is essential to true balance, and represents more of an opposite than necessarily a negative. It is a vital part of maintaining balance throughout the universe.

References: Death, mourning, slimming and/or elegant fashion, evil, traditional dress, Halloween

Spells: Ward off negativity, protection from evil, moving from negative to positive influences, cleansing, removal of spells and/or discord, grief, truth, justice, authority

Blue

A soothing shade of blue can produce chemicals in the body that create a natural calming effect. Therefore, the color blue is associated with healing, boosting intuition, and initiating a serene, calm nature. Electric blues that are more shocking and brilliant, however, work the opposite way, causing exhilaration. Statistically, blue has often been found to be the favorite color of both men and women.

Chakra: Fifth

References: Blue mood (depression), tranquility, sky and sea, royalty, Fourth of July (with white and red)

Spells: Healing, peace, safe journey/travel, self-expression, writing

Brown

A conservative color, brown represents both nature and hearth and home. Those who prefer this color tend to be reliable, stable, and content.

References: Nature, dirt, Thanksgiving

Spells: Home and hearth, stability, family, animal health

Gold

Like yellow, gold represents high energy and optimism. It's also a great color to represent wealth (as in the mineral gold) and good fortune, as well as dignity and wisdom.

References: Prosperity, gold rush, sunlight, royalty, Mardi Gras (with earthy green and mystical purple)

Spells: Good fortune, achievement, business success

Gray

Although associated with negative connotations such as a gray sky or a gray mood, this neutral color mixes well with any other color. Gray can be used for business success or to develop focus, but because of its noncommittal nature, gray may have less potency than other colors. Also, "gray matter" refers to the brain, indicating intelligence.

References Neutrality, stability, "gray matter"

Spells: Focus, business Success, going the long haul

Green

Green represents the natural world, is a symbol of the environmental movement, and is now a buzzword for all things ecological. However, green also represents the almighty dollar and the lure of wealth and success. The color should be used for attracting wealth and good fortune, and also for conjuring fertility or a good harvest, and anything connected with gardening and nature. Green is a well-balanced color and is believed to be the luckiest color in the Western world. Use it to attract good fortune and luck.

Chakra: Fourth

References: Money, jealousy, nature, ecology, Christmas (with red), Mardi Gras (with abundant gold and mystical purple). Green is "the symbolic color of the astral plane, being the plane of growth through desire," according to the *Dictionary of All Scriptures and Myths.*

Spells: Wealth, abundance, good luck, fertility, employment, changing direction, healing, growth, agriculture/gardening, rebirth, confidence, hope

Indigo

This deep shade of blue represents the more spiritual side of the color blue. It produces the same calming effects, and also delves into the dream world and the balance between the human body and the outer realms.

Chakra: Sixth

References: Peace, indigo bunting, indigo children

Spells: Healing, dreams, truth, protection, balancing higher and lower selves or bodies with the universe, clarity

Orange

Depending on the shade, orange can be warm and inviting or overstimulating. It represents the warmth and vitality of the sun, and also its abundant energy that never ends. Its influence will vary as it veers closer to red (stimulating and passionate) or yellow (warmer but lively).

Chakra: Second

References: Autumn, warning, Orange Irish, Halloween, Thanksgiving

Spells: Self-expression, creativity, joy, endurance, strength, vitality

Pink (also Rose)

The color that represents the feminine side of life, pink is perfect for emotional spells such as attracting romantic love and friendship. The color invokes feelings of safety, emotional comfort, and a caring heart.

References: Girls, bubble gum, "pretty in pink," breast cancer awareness, Easter

Spells: Romantic love, friendship, emotions, nurturing

Purple

Mystical and mysterious, purple symbolizes royalty in some cultures. The color is a combination of red and blue, an actual marrying of the attributes of stimulation and calm, and invokes feelings of mysticism and creativity and a sense of power. It also represents wisdom. Purple and violet gris gris bags are a good choice for creating spells for creative people.

References: "Purple prose," "purple heart," spirituality, Mardi Gras (with abundant gold and earthy green)

Spells: Ambition, power, spiritual development, intuition, repelling negativity, wisdom

Red

Red stimulates the life force, even though the color has the lowest frequency of visible light. It can represent danger and caution (think of red stop signs and traffic lights) or passion and romance. Red is an emotional color and full of vibrant energy, perfect for sexuality, energy, and strength. If romantic love is your mission, pink may be a better, more stable, place to start. Red has been credited with warding off evil.

Chakra: First (base chakra)

References: Valentine's Day, Christmas (with earthy green), heart, passion, strength, vitality, devil (in Western culture), Fourth of July (with white and blue)

Spells: Sexuality, passion, vitality, stamina, energy, strength, focus, enthusiasm, courage, success

Silver

Like gold, silver represents money and wealth. Its more ethereal and optimistic side ("Every cloud has a silver lining") can be used to initiate psychic development in a person or to provide spiritual enlightenment and insight.

References: Money, New Year's Eve, "silver lining," moon energy

Spells: Clairvoyance, psychic development, balance, success, insight

Violet

Artistic and creative people relate to the color violet. As the seventh chakra, it represents the connection between the human body and the spiritual realm. Violet also promotes passion and sensuality, and is a good color for protection charms.

Chakra: Seventh

References: African violets

Spells: Self-improvement, unity between self and universe, spiritual healing, psychic power, protection, intelligence.

White

Perhaps because white is the combination of all colors within the spectrum, it represents birth, purity, and protection. As with the winter solstice and the return of the sun, the white colors of winter signify rebirth or the beginning of a new cycle. Many practitioners visualize white light around objects and people as a cocoon of protection. It is believed that imagining a white light going toward a malevolent energy or person will keep them at a distance.

References: Purity, birth, weddings, "the Great White Way," spirit at death/"white light," Fourth of July (with red and blue)

Spells: Happiness, joy, purity, protection, peace, truth, life's pathway

Yellow

Yellow is a bright attention-getter, producing a warm lively feeling in its viewer. Those who wear yellow are usually full of energy, optimism, and creative spark. This color stimulates the viewer and should be used for bags that promote mental alertness as part of the charm. Yellow is also effective for divination, stimulating psychic powers and enhancing spiritual wisdom.

Chakra: Third

References: Sunlight, happiness, yellow ribbons for returning soldiers, Easter

Spells: Understanding, persuasion, creativity, mental alertness, learning, teaching, happiness, wisdom, divination

> *The use of expressive colors is felt to be one of the basic elements of the modern mentality, an historical necessity, beyond choice.*
> —Henri Matisse

Making the Bag

Red flannel was the fabric of choice among voodoo conjurers wishing to create a spell bag—a gris gris, mojo, root bag, conjure hand, lucky hand, etc.—that would manifest desires or provide protection. Leather, chamois, and other materials were also used for bags, particularly among Native Americans and Europeans.

Today, small bags made out of a variety of materials can be purchased at hobby stores, party stores, fabric shops, and online, and most come with an attached drawstring to pull it closed. Manufactured bags come in various sizes, the choice of which is completely up to you. Some are made of lightweight material, allowing you to see the items inside the bag (which is helpful if you include charms, talismans, or other objects that reinforce your intention when you gaze upon them). Keep in mind, however, that mesh, organza, or other sheer bags will sift fine powdered herbs and spices through them. Other fabrics, like flannel, felt, cotton, or even heartier materials like canvas, will prohibit this. Again, the choice of fabric is yours, but make sure that its color corresponds to the intention you wish to bring forth in your gris gris. For instance, use a pink bag for love spells, a green bag for prosperity spells, and a violet bag for protection spells.

Manufactured bags for your gris gris are widely available.

To make a gris gris bag or spell sachet by hand, first choose the color that corresponds to your intention. Once you have chosen the right color, select your fabric (most fabric stores sell small pieces of felt in an assortment of colors, which are perfect for making gris gris bags). Draw a circle, about seven to nine inches in diameter, on the fabric—placing a bowl upside-down on the fabric and tracing around the rim will make it easier to create a perfect circle. After the circle is drawn, cut it out with your scissors. You now have a round piece of fabric.

Using your scissors, prick several holes in the fabric about a half-inch from the edge, all around the circle's perimeter. These will be used for the string that binds your bag together. Choose your string, leather, or ribbon and weave it through the holes, going in and out so that when you pull the string tight, the bag will close up.

Bead lovers might wish to make a beaded bag (Native Americans created many of their medicine bags this way), and quilters may assemble several fabrics to form a unique quilted bag. If you incorporate a long heavy string, such as leather or twine, you can hang your gris gris bag from your rear-view mirror. (Note that in some states this is against the law, since it may obstruct the driver's view).

Choosing Candles

The use of candles in religious ceremonies is a centuries-old tradition. The light of a candle represents a spiritual force of illumination and divine light, and gives a peaceful glow of clarity, tranquility, and wisdom. The type and color of the candles you burn while making your gris gris bag are up to you, and you can choose the colors of your candles based on your spell's intention (just as you choose the color for your bag).

While one or more candles may be used, we suggest using three candles. It's always good to light a white candle, since white is the universal color of protection, along with a candle whose color matches your spell (such as a green candle for prosperity or a pink candle for love). We also recommend lighting a black candle, which is a way to offer acknowledgment and appreciation of the role dark energy plays in the balance of the universe and in spell creation. (This helps keep malevolent energies at bay, since merely denying the existence of underworld energy leaves one unprepared for the possibility of it influencing the spell; acknowledging this energy maintains balance.)

Here is a brief list of candle colors and their associations:

Black: Justice, protection, truth, overall protection, alternative energy

Blue: Healing, inspiration, peace, wisdom, dream magic, restful sleep

Brown: Animals, family, home and hearth, safe dwelling

Gold: Achievement, good fortune, success, wealth, progress and renewal

Gray: Business success, focus, regrouping

Green: Employment, fertility, good luck, prosperity, rebirth, money, Earth energy

Orange: Creativity, endurance, joy, justice, resolve

Pink: Friendship, true love, nurturing

Purple: Ambition, power, spiritual development, psychic powers

Red: Courage, life force, passion, strength, success, battles

Silver: Balance, clairvoyance, psychic powers, moon energy

White: Peace, purity, universal guidance and protection, cleansing, friendship

Yellow: Creativity, happiness, imagination, wisdom, divination, ancestral connection

Now that you have your candles and your bag, you can collect your ingredients, light your candles, and begin the assembly.

Assembling the Bag

Before you begin to assemble, it's essential that you purify your sacred space. When we say "sacred," it does not mean that you are traveling to Lourdes or Stonehenge, but that you are creating a quiet, peaceful spot in your home or business as your sanctified area in which to create gris gris bags. If you own an altar, by all means utilize this sacred space. If your kitchen table makes the best assembling spot, do not hesitate to set up shop and get to work. We use our kitchen tables for creating gris gris and find that these surfaces resonate with healing energy, due to their function as family gathering places and because they exist in the center of our homes.

To purify your space, first give it a good cleaning. Nothing hinders positive energies more than a dirty table top. Once you have a clean surface, consider burning incense, juniper leaves, or sage, and using cedar smudge sticks to purify the area. Using a broom to brush away negativity works as well. You may use a ceremonial broom or the old-fashioned kind, but the bristles don't have to touch the ground. Merely making circling motions with your broom as if to cleanse the space of its negativity will suffice.

Once you have found a safe place to assemble your ingredients— such as an altar, table, or space outside devoid of wind—and once the area is cleansed and purified, place the ingredients before you: herbs, stones, bones, shells and charms, etc. In the third part of this book, you will learn which spells require which items and what each of the items means.

Ingredients for your bag may include various herbs, nuts, stones, and shells.

Place a candle in the center of your workspace, making sure its color matches the spell, and light it, saying, "Bless this space and all power brought forth." Ask the universe to guide you in your quest. You may wish to call upon a higher power—be it God, Goddess, patron deities, spirit guides, or other guardians—to guide you in your endeavor. Ask for their blessings and assistance.

If you're uncomfortable asking in your own words or cannot find the right words, here's one incantation you may wish to use: "Universal spirits, God, Goddess, and universal divine wisdom, protect this space with your white light of protection and grant me insight to make good choices and to bring about the object of my desire."

Most people create gris gris bags for themselves, but if you assemble a bag for another it's helpful to carve the person's name into the spell-colored candle or place a photo of the person nearby, so that you can gaze upon their face while assembling the ingredients. In our experience, bags made for others out of love have an extra edge toward success.

Now it's time to assemble the bag. While the herbs, stones, and other ingredients inherent to each spell are listed in Part III, the final selection of items for your bag is up to you, based purely on your particular intention. Once you select the ingredients you wish to use—such as lemon verbena, primrose, rosehips, rosemary, and rose quartz for a love spell, or basil, cinquefoil, cloves, sage, pecan, a silver coin, green jade, lodestone, and a cowrie shell for a prosperity spell—put these ingredients into your bag. Remember that you should pick an odd number of items.

As you place each ingredient in the bag, thank the plant, tree, flower, stone, or animal for its assistance on your behalf. It is essential to maintain focus during this time. Never lose sight of your intention, especially while you handle the ingredients. This can be an exciting experience, especially if you take your time handling the herbs and taking in their aromas, imagine the history of each plant along with its properties, and share in its energies.

While you assemble your gris gris, it's preferable to ask for what you want aloud, such as "I assemble these herbs and stones and ask for prosperity" or "I call love to me with these herbs, stones, and a lock of my true love's hair." Many of the spells in this book contain chants for you to use. For example, if you are creating a cleansing bag, banishing negativity in your life, or hoping to eliminate bad habits, here is Jude's chant for the waning moon. After assembling the bag, speak these words aloud every night of the waning moon, with the last line recited with passion and directed toward the new moon when it arrives.

> *It is this night, a night so dark*
> *the waning moon takes away*
> *and banished will be evil's mark*
> *and only shall good fortune stay*
> *Upon this moon, once cleansed and black*
> *without light and without voice*
> *I shed the curse to suffer lack*
> *and am now blessed with the power of choice*
> *For when the clock face passes peak*
> *and the sleeping moon awakens*
> *then so the power feeds the meek*
> *and all sorrow is forsaken*
> *prosperity I call down*

If you feel uncomfortable saying your intentions aloud, write them down or just visualize the gris gris bag working on your behalf. You may also wish to write your intention on a piece of paper and either include it in the bag or burn it within the candle's flame upon the bag's completion.

Once you finish placing the ingredients in the bag, it's time to pull the strings closed. Your gris gris bag is now complete. Keep your candles lit until this point. If you incorporated a written intention as part of your spell, such as writing a loved one's name on a piece of paper while constructing the bag, you may read it aloud and then burn it in the candle flame to seal the spell.

Once the bag is created, thank the universe and Mother Nature for their assistance, and blow out the flame.

You may wish to embellish the outside of your bag with additional corresponding elements, such as a sprig of rosemary or a piece of willow attached by copper, of course depending upon your intention. Charms make wonderful embellishments, and you can purchase these at hobby stores or find them lying around the house. A single earring, with its mate missing, can make for a nice addition to the outside of your bag. An earring containing hearts may be sewn onto the outside of a love gris gris. Other bits of broken jewelry can serve as talismans, like the natural talismans discussed later in this book. Our favorite embellishments involve twisted willow, braided copper wire, or antler coins, since they infuse various elements—tree, metal, animal—into your bag.

Include charms that are meaningful to you or add to the intention of the bag.

Let your imagination soar. The essential ingredient, above all, is faith. Nearly everything accomplished in this world and the next requires the simple belief that it can be so.

Are you ready? The following chapters list a wide variety of spells; the appropriate days of the week and month in which to cast them; a list of herbs, stones, and other items to include; and a few pieces of advice. Let's get started.

Charms can be sewn on, glued on, or woven on.

General Guidelines

Here is a quick reference guide to keep handy while assembling a gris gris bag:

1. Always express gratitude as you create your bag.
2. Remember the law of three—that which is put out into the universe will return to you threefold. Never build a bag with negative intention.
3. When creating a bag for someone else, always ask their permission and try to involve them in the process.
4. Never force your beliefs on another.
5. Remember to honor nature in all you do. Never take the life of, or injure, an animal to create your bag. Choose your plants and stones carefully, and never remove anything from protected areas.
6. As you gather your items, always give thanks to the universe and Mother Earth for their bounty.
7. Be cautious with your plants, herbs, and spices. Some can be toxic. Research what you choose for your bag and always keep your blends away from children and animals. Even nontoxic items can sicken a small child or pet.

8. Be aware of allergies in yourself, your family, and the bag's recipient.

9. Understand your responsibility. Magic is a powerful thing. Don't dabble.

10. Be careful what you wish for. When we talk about being specific with your intentions, it is not only to make your bag effective, but to avoid any unwelcome results.

11. Avoid bending the will of another.

Your gris gris bag is complete, and its energy is at work.

part two

Ingredients

NATURE WITHIN YOUR BAG

· · · · · · · · · · · · · · ·

Aristotle said, "In <u>all things of nature, there is something of the</u> <u>marvelous</u>."

As new technology improves communication, transforms the workplace, and relieves housework, our lives become easier—and yet we move further away from nature. As always, however, nature remains steadfast in all its glory, waiting for us to seek its wisdom.

The ingredients described in this section—herbs, roots, flowers, trees, stones, crystals, metals, shells, bones, talismans—can be used in the creation of gris gris bags and spell sachets. Mystical powers have long been attributed to these items, but this list is by no means complete. We have chosen those described here for their sacred associations, easy attainability, and commonality.

Trees, for instance, are an ever-present part of our lives, even within large cities. It's hard not to feel connected to trees; Henry David Thoreau spent two years living simply among the forests of Walden Pond, writing, "I frequently tramped eight or ten miles through the deepest snow to keep an appointment with a beech tree, or a yellow birch, or an old acquaintance among the pines." Trees were considered sacred by the ancient Druids, who met and held ceremonies in sacred groves throughout Europe. Some species were more revered than others, and the most-honored twenty-five trees became associated with symbols (runes) in the early medieval Ogham alphabet. This system of parallel lines, used primarily to write Old Irish, has many layers to it and is replete with mystery; while not every letter in the Ogham alphabet is attributable to a tree, the system is often referred to as the "Celtic Tree Alphabet" since some of the symbols can be read as indicating a specific tree's usefulness or magical essence.

We associate flowers with joy and inspiration. Camellias blooming in winter make us think of endurance and health. Marigolds, with their long blooming season, are associated with longevity. Some Asian traditions associate the lotus with purity, while the Hindus saw its unfolding petals as a symbol of the expansion of the soul, so it's no wonder the lotus represents spiritual growth and rebirth.

Herbs have long been a way to add culinary accents and aid healing and magic, with evidence of this dating as far back as the ancient Egyptians and Native Americans. Throughout history, few people grew gardens without adding an ample supply of herbs, both to flavor the foods they ate and to heal the sick.

Some herbs contain simple magic that is easily explained. Lavender, for instance, with its sweet aroma, induces sleep, and thus is used in bags and dream pillows to trigger sweet dreams. Other herbs, such as the little-known betony, were associated with protection and repelling negativity and therefore planted in churchyards and carried in pouches.

Bring the magical attributes of herbs, trees, flowers, and other plants into your gris gris bags and spell sachets, casting their power forth for yourself or for others. Please always remember that plants are living beings, whose purpose is to aid us on our journeys. Give thanks to Mother Earth for their creation as you choose them for your bags. Be thankful that the magic of the universe exists in these living organisms, and that this divine association connects us to a higher being—one who will bring us good fortune.

> *Does magic really work? Can plants help you find love and create abundance? The answer to those questions is a resounding yes.... Plants are alive and full of their own unique energy. As you learn to align yourself with their energy, anything is possible.*
> —Susan Gregg, *The Complete Illustrated Encyclopedia of Magical Plants*

HERBS

. . . .

Ever since ancient times, herbalists have studied and written about plants that heal. The ancient Chinese *Canon of Herbs* lists 252 plants and their associations with human consumption, and the Egyptians used herbs for cosmetics as well as medicine. The Bible and the sacred Ayurvedas of India contain numerous references to both medicinal and magical plants. The Greek physician Dioscorides mentioned six hundred healing plants in his *De Materia Medica* (first century A.D.).

The most famous books written about herbs are Nicholas Culpeper's *The English Physician* and the *Complete Herbal*, published in 1652 and 1653, which examine hundreds of species of plants and include information on their astrological properties. John Gerard and John Parkinson, also Elizabethan herbalists, both catalogued more than a thousand species.

Along with the study of the medicinal qualities of plants, there were numerous superstitions and legends. Some were based on mythology, and some were directly associated with the plant's attributes.

Here are some of the most common herbs used in gris gris bags:

Aconite/Wolfbane

One of the most common names for aconite is wolf's bane or wolfbane, due to hunters using this herb on the tip of their spears when hunting wolves. Its generic name, *aconitum napellus*, could be derived from *akontion*, Latin for "dart," or *akone*, which means "rocky" (the plant is sometimes found on cliffs and in rocky terrain).

Aconite is deadly toxic, which is said to be due to its being slobbered on by Cerberus, the three-headed dog guarding the entrance to Hades. Other Greek myths mention aconite as a love poison; Medea poisoned Theseus with aconite. Later legends claim that witches mixed aconite with belladonna in order to fly.

Other names for aconite, especially prominent during Shakespeare's time, include "helmet flower" or "monkshood," due to the flap on top of the flower that falls over the rest of the bloom.

Use in Gris Gris Bags for:
Protection

In the Garden:
Aconite is a hardy perennial but highly poisonous. It prefers rich and somewhat moist soil, such as a moist loam, and partial shade.

Additional Uses:
As a medicine, aconite decreases blood pressure and reduces inflammation.

Interesting Fact:
The aconite root may be mistaken for horseradish and its leaves for parsley. Because of these similarities, it's wise not to grow aconite in a kitchen garden.

Anise

Talk about a versatile herb. Anise not only aids digestion, calms coughs and asthma, dispels intestinal discomfort, and relieves gas, but it freshens a person's breath as well.

The Romans used anise in a cake called *mustaceum*, which was usually served after big meals like marriage ceremonies. The cake, which aided digestion and no doubt cleared the room of bad breath, may be the ancestor of the modern wedding cake.

Anise is also used to make licorice-flavored candy and is a key ingredient in the notorious German herbal liqueur, Jagermeister.

Use in Gris Gris Bags for:
Love, protection, purification

In the Garden:
Anise is an annual that prefers a long dry season to seed (it requires 70 degree temperatures to germinate).

Additional Uses:
For years, anise was effectively used as a lure in mousetraps.

Interesting Fact:
Dogs adore this herb, much like cats prefer catnip.

Basil

The French call basil the *herbe royale*. In Italy, basil is a sign of love. Old Louisiana folklore holds that planting basil on either side of a doorstep will result in good luck for the homeowner. And those who place basil in their pockets in Mexico will attract money, or their lover's eye will cease roving.

Basil is thought to be native to India, but it has been found in ancient Asia and Africa as well. It enjoys a rich history with the goddess Tulasi in India, where it is used to swear oaths in court. Story has it that basil was found growing around Christ's tomb, and some Greek Orthodox churches use basil beneath their altars. In Haiti, basil belongs to the goddess Erzulie.

Use in Gris Gris Bags for:
Happiness, love, peace, prosperity, protection, repelling negativity

In the Garden:
Basil is extremely easy to grow. Plant seeds in pots indoors until the threat of frost has passed, then transplant to the garden. Pinch leaves at the base of stems for use.

Additional Uses:
In Italy, women place a pot of basil on a windowsill to show the world they are ready for a suitor. Basil leaves can be carried in your pocket for protection, or dried and used in many culinary dishes.

Interesting Fact:
The ancient Greeks and Romans planted basil while ranting and raving, believing that these tirades would help the herb grow. The

expression "to rant and rave" in French is *semer le basilic*, literally meaning, "to sow the basil."[17]

Bergamot

American bergamot (not to be confused with bergamot orange, the citrus) grows throughout the eastern half of the United States. Also known as scarlet bee balm, it attracts bees and hummingbirds. The Oswego Indians of New York used the herb in teas and taught this technique to colonial Boston residents, who drank bergamot tea in lieu of the real thing after they dumped the highly taxed tea imported from England into Boston harbor.

The Lakotas also used the herb in tea form to fight fevers, colds, and whooping coughs, as bergamot contains the antiseptic thymol. Other Native Americans employed bergamot to treat nasal congestion, insect bites, and flatulence, along with other ailments.

Use bergamot's dried flowers and leaves in gris gris bags when you need clarity on an issue.

Use in Gris Gris Bags for:
Clarity

In the Garden:
Plant in sun or part shade in rich, light, or moist soil.

Additional Uses:
The dried flowers bring a lemony fragrance to potpourris.

Interesting Fact:
The early Shakers used bergamot as a medicinal tea and also in cooking.

Betony

Betony has numerous medicinal qualities, but it is best known for its protective attributes. Not only was the herb planted in churchyards to dispel evil, but some wore the herb in a bag around the neck to

---

17. Jack Staub, *75 Exceptional Herbs for Your Garden* (Layton, UT: Gibb Smith, 2008).

further protect themselves from harm. Others found betony good for warding off bad visions and dreams. One of the nine sacred herbs,[18] Betony was also used as an Anglo-Saxon protective charm.

The Dutch theologian Erasmus recommended wearing betony in some form for "driving away devils and despair" and said that it was "good against fearful visions."[19]

Use in Gris Gris Bags for:
Repelling evil and negativity, strength, sweet dreams

In the Garden:
This tall, purple-flowering perennial prefers rich, well-drained soil and sun or part shade.

Additional Uses:
Steeped, dried betony leaves make a delicious tea.

Interesting Fact:
The Italians say, "Sell your coat and buy betony," and the Spaniards say, "He has as many virtues as betony."

Black Hellebore

Black hellebore blooms from late December through March and sometimes at Christmastime, which gave it the nickname "Christmas rose." This hearty herb was also labeled "protective" for defying the harsh nature of winter. Black hellebore flowers were placed on thresholds and on farm animals to ward off evil and protect from harm.

Although it has been used medicinally, black hellebore is poisonous.

Use in Gris Gris Bags for:
Contacting spirits, repelling negativity

---

18. The nine sacred herbs are usually identified as mugwort, plantain, watercress, *atterlothe* (understood as betony, sometimes as sainfoin), chamomile, nettle, crab apple, chervil, and fennel. Thyme is sometimes considered part of this list.

19. Jack Staub, op. cit.

In the Garden:
This perennial prefers rich, well-drained soil in partial shade to full sun.

Additional Uses:
Black hellebore makes a nice winter flower in your garden, but wear gloves when handling it; the leaves contain poison.

Interesting Fact:
The herb has a black root, which is where it gets its name.

Blackberry

Blackberries make wonderful summer pies, but they also healed gout in ancient Greece and were used in poultices for burns in England. Native Americans used blackberries as a tonic to improve circulation and an astringent to cure dysentery.

Wild blackberry bushes can be found just about anywhere, from railroad tracks and roadsides to formal backyards. Use the leaves in your spell bags.

Use in Gris Gris Bags for:
Healing, prosperity, protection

In the Garden:
Blackberry vines prefer moist, moderately rich soil in full sun to part shade.

Additional Uses:
A summer just isn't summer without blackberry pies, cobblers, and other sweets, plus delicious blackberry wine.

Interesting Fact:
Thornless blackberry vines are now available.

Black Cohosh

Black cohosh is native to North America and grows in eastern deciduous forests. Native Americans used the herb's roots for gynecological ailments, primarily menstrual problems and to ease childbirth.

Today, formulas for premenstrual ailments and menopausal symptoms contain black cohosh because the herb may help to balance estrogen, although it takes a while for the healing properties to kick in (up to four weeks). In addition, black cohosh is known to relieve muscle strain, leg cramps, and stomach spasms.

Use in Gris Gris Bags for:
Courage, love, protection

In the Garden:
Black cohosh is a hardy perennial that grows from southern Canada to the Atlantic and down to Georgia, preferring moist, rich soil in shaded areas.

Additional Uses:
Other names for the herb include "bugbane" and "bugwort" because it is thought to repel insects.

Interesting Fact:
Black cohosh is a member of the buttercup family.

Black-Eyed Peas

On New Year's Day, Southerners traditionally cook up a dish made of black-eyed peas and greens (or cabbage). Called Hoppin' John and served over rice, this dish is thought to attract wealth—the peas resemble coins, while the greens resemble money. The rice, which swells in cooking, is also thought to encourage prosperity.[20]

So it's natural that a few black-eyed peas be added to the mix in a prosperity bag.

---

20. Andrew F. Smith, *Oxford Encyclopedia of Food and Drink in America* (New York: Oxford University Press, 1976).

Use in Gris Gris Bags for:
Luck, prosperity

In the Garden:
Black-eyed peas enjoy Southern climes without the threat of frost. Be sure to check zone listings to make sure they can grow in your area.

Additional Uses:
Set a pot of black-eyed peas on the stove while constructing your bags—with or without meat and seasonings—and you'll have a tasty meal later.

Interesting Fact:
Black-eyed peas are commonly used in Greek cooking.

Caraway Seeds

Explorers have found caraway seeds in excavations as old as 4000 B.C., and the seeds are mentioned in the Bible. Caraway has also been traced back to Egypt and the old Silk Road, and may very well be the oldest-known herb. Its name derives from the Arabic *karawya*, meaning "seed."

In the first century A.D., Dioscorides recommended doses of caraway for pale-faced girls. The soldiers of Valerius ate the seeds, and in Shakespeare's *Henry IV*, Squire Shallow offers Flagstaff a roasted apple with caraway seeds after a meal.

The seeds, with their licorice-flavored qualities, are used to flavor breads, soups, cheese, and cakes. Caraway has also been used as an additive to birdfeed, and people who raise birds swear their birds never fly away when eating these seeds. Caraway became synonymous with love potions, because it was thought that anyone who ate the seeds would not wander.

To protect children from sickness and harm, place a bag of caraway seeds under a child's crib or bed.[21]

---

21. Susan Gregg, *The Complete Illustrated Encyclopedia of Magical Plants* (Beverly, MA: Fair Winds, 2008).

Use in Gris Gris Bags for:
Love, protection (for children), repelling negativity, retention

In the Garden:
Plant in rich loam and full sun.

Additional Uses:
A tea made of caraway seeds may help eliminate colic in babies.

Interesting Fact:
It was once thought that caraway seeds pounded into a poultice would heal bruises.

Catnip

Catnip has been around for centuries. It was familiar to the Romans, the Europeans, and American writers like Washington Irving, Nathaniel Hawthorne, and Harriet Beecher Stowe. Although most people think of the herb as a feline treat, it has been used medicinally for sore throats, anxiety, digestive complaints, and headaches, and also as a sleeping tonic, most commonly as a tea.

Catnip contains nepetalactone, a chemical that drives cats wild with pleasure when they inhale it. Not all cats succumb to catnip, however. About 25 percent can resist this alluring herb. Humans, alas, don't receive the same effect from catnip, and can only watch as their felines roll around in ecstasy. But nepetalactone is known to repel cockroaches and mosquitoes, so grow it in your garden to keep both yourself and your cat happy, in your own individual ways.

Use in Gris Gris Bags for:
Beauty, happiness, love, pets (good health for your cat)

In the Garden:
Catnip is hardy, preferring well-drained soil but tolerant of just about anything else. For a more fragrant herb, plant in sandy soil and full sun. If you want to see your catnip babies grow up, place behind shrubs or fences to keep cats away.

Additional Uses:
Catnip can be used as a flavoring in sauces and soups.

Interesting Fact:
Catnip was the preferred tea of the English before Chinese tea took over the market.

Cayenne

When people hear of cayenne pepper, they think of Cajun and Creole cooking or a spicy dish from Latin America. Although cayenne has been used in these cuisines, it also enhances the foods of Southeast Asia, China, and Southern Italy.

Cayenne not only spices up food but helps to stimulate the blood by opening capillaries and, believe it or not, aids the digestive system. Cayenne also helps to ward off colds and is a great source of vitamins C and A, in addition to antioxidant-rich flavonoids and carotenoids.

The pepper has been used for centuries for its medicinal qualities, due to its pain-relieving chemical, capsaicin. Native Americans, traditional Indian Ayurvedics, Chinese, Japanese, and Koreans have used the pepper for digestive and circulatory problems. Today, a capsaicin cream is used extensively to relieve the pain associated with arthritis, shingles, back pain, and psoriasis.

And of course, the bottles found floating in the Vermilion River in Lafayette, Louisiana, containing papers with good riddance spells, occasionally contained cayenne. The herb, given its firepower, can be used to push people away as well as to instill and attract passion.

Use in Gris Gris Bags for:
Good riddance, passion

In the Garden:
Plant cayenne in a warm, sunny climate, preferably in tropical and subtropical areas. The herb may be grown indoors, but with bright light from a southern exposure.

Additional Uses:

Some studies have shown that cayenne raises a person's body heat, thus causing weight loss. Breaking out into a sweat in fact cools the body off and helps purge a flu or cold.

Interesting Fact:

Cayenne is derived from a Greek word meaning "to bite."

Chamomile

This lovely smelling herb, used by the ancient Egyptians for "agues" or malarial chills and placed in Roman baths to cure weariness, was one of the Anglo-Saxon nine sacred herbs.

Chamomile is best known, however, for its soothing qualities as a tea. It's used for digestive ailments and anxiety, and as a sleeping aid. Even Peter Rabbit's mother brewed the tea for her famous literary son.

"A cup of chamomile tea is a classic remedy for nervous or hysterical conditions." The herb can also be placed in bath water to "calm irritable or hyperactive children."[22]

Use in Gris Gris Bags for:

Happiness, prosperity, purification, repelling negativity, sweet (or prophetic) dreams

In the Garden:

There are two types of chamomile: Roman or common chamomile, a low-growing perennial, and German or wild chamomile, a tall annual. Both are widely cultivated and enjoy full sun to partial shade. Roman chamomile prefers light, dry soil and German chamomile prefers a sandy, well-drained soil.

Additional Uses:

Chamomile was "strewn" in medieval England to mask the unpleasant odors rising from unbathed bodies.

---

22. Gaea and Shandor Weiss, *Growing and Using Healing Herbs* (Emmaus, PA: Rodale, 1985).

Interesting Fact:

The herb releases its scent when crushed. An English ditty says,

> *"Like a chamomile bed*
> *the more it is trodden*
> *the more it will spread"*

Chervil

Native to Russia and the Middle East, this herb was found in Tutankhamun's tomb in Egypt. It traveled from Rome into France, where it became one of the traditional "fine herbs." The herb's oils caused some to call it "myrrhis" because of its resemblance to myrrh. For that reason, and for its restorative properties, chervil soup is served on Maundy Thursday during Easter.

The name "chervil" is derived from the Greek that means "leaves of joy."

Use in Gris Gris Bags for:

Repelling negativity (as one of the Anglo-Saxon nine sacred herbs), youth

In the Garden:

This hardy annual prefers a cool, regularly watered shady area.

Additional Uses:

Some believe that chewing chervil cures hiccups.

Interesting Fact:

Chervil is full of bioflavonoids.

Chicory

There are many stories as to why New Orleans residents love chicory in their coffee. The French, most notably, have used chicory as a coffee substitution or enhancer for years, which may account for its popularity in the Big Easy. Another story has it that the Civil War blockade of New Orleans caused residents to add chicory to their coffee to make it go further, since coffee beans were scarce. Whatever the reason, New Orleanians love their chicory coffee.

Chicory leaves are used in cooking, and the herb's medicinal qualities have been labeled as a tonic, laxative, and diuretic, which may account for its magical uses as a cleansing herb and one that removes obstacles. Because chicory is used to cleanse or remove, creating bags with chicory should be done during a waning moon.

Use in Gris Gris Bags for:
Overcoming obstacles, purification

In the Garden:
This wild weed grows in pastures and fields and produces blue flowers. In the garden, use a deep bed and give it plenty of room.

Additional Uses:
Farm animals can be fed chicory to battle internal parasites.

Interesting Fact:
In European folklore, chicory can open locked doors.

Cinquefoil (Five-Leaf Grass)

Cinquefoil has a history of magical connotations. It was believed to have been used in flying potions and is found in old grimoires, sometimes by the name "fingers." It is said that if you hang cinquefoil over a doorway, it will protect the house. Bathe in the herb, and it washes away hexes and purifies. Place a sprig of seven leaflets of cinquefoil within a dream sachet and place it beneath your pillow to dream of a future lover or mate, or hang a gris gris bag containing cinquefoil from your bedpost to ensure a restful sleep.

According to Mrs. Grieve's *A Modern Herbal*, cinquefoil was used to cure fevers, especially in marshy, ill-drained lands. Dioscorides believed that "one leaf cured a quotidian, three a tertian and four a quarten ague." The plant's five leaflets represent love, money, health, power, and wisdom, and can be used in appropriate spells. Voodoo legend has it that a gris gris bag of cinquefoil will help its owner win a court case by gaining favor with the judge.

Use in Gris Gris Bags for:

Fortune in court cases, healing, love, prophetic dreams, prosperity, protection, purification, sweet dreams, wisdom

In the Garden:

Plant this perennial in full sun or partial shade in moderate climates.

Additional Uses:

Cinquefoil root was used to produce a red dye, and the top of the herb was used as an astringent and mouthwash.

Interesting Fact:

Cinquefoil was used as a special bait in fishing; it serves as the patron herb of fishermen.

Clover

Legends abound about clover, particularly the four-leaf clovers that are thought to be lucky charms.

In Ireland, the three-leaved white clover is known as the shamrock and used as the emblem of sports teams, tourism, and Aer Lingus airlines. The shamrock got its name and honor because its leaves represented a trinity. Even though this is a revered Christian symbol, it is thought the Druids honored the plant for its trifoliate as well.

Use in Gris Gris Bags for:

Protection (three-leaved clover); to avoid military service, to strengthen psychic powers, to sense the presence of spirits, to attract prosperity (four-leaved clover); prosperity (five-leaved clover); expelling negativity (white clover); passion or to expel negativity (red clover)

In the Garden:

A spring and summer perennial with hundreds of varieties, clover is believed to repel snakes wherever it grows, which is usually everywhere in the wild. You can grow white clover from seed, and it should be planted in well-drained moist soil in full to moderate sun. Clover makes a great alternative to grass lawns.

Additional Uses:

Clover was a popular motif in Victorian times and is part of several flags and coat of arms, including the Erin Go Bragh flag.

Interesting Fact:

The scientific name, *trifolium* or trefoil, derives from the Latin *tres* meaning "three" and *folium* meaning "leaf."

Comfrey

For centuries, herbalists and physicians have used the comfrey root to heal wounds, cuts, and broken bones. And they were on to something. Comfrey roots promotes cell multiplication that makes wounds and bones heal faster.

There was a time when mistaken but hopeful women bathed in comfrey or drank its tea to restore virginity, but modern medicine has found the herb to be too toxic to use internally.

Use in Gris Gris Bags for:

Prosperity, safe travel

In the Garden:

Plant in rich soil in full sun.

Additional Uses:

The plant's oil can be used to treat skin irritations such as eczema.

Interesting Fact:

Comfrey has more protein in its leaves than any other vegetable.

Dandelion

What looks like the lawn's most obnoxious weed is actually a plant chock-full of medicinal qualities. The dandelion contains vast amounts of beta-carotene for fighting cancer, vitamins A, B, C, and D, and a host of minerals. In fact, dandelion boasts the highest amount of vitamin A of any plant! Makes you think twice about pulling it up, doesn't it?

You can consume all parts of the dandelion. Its leaves are great in salads, and the roots and flower delicious in a variety of preparations. A tea brewed from dandelion is believed to enhance psychic powers. The word "dandelion" comes from the Old French *dent de lion*, literally meaning "the teeth of the lion."

Use in Gris Gris Bags for:

Calling spirits, home and hearth, love, peace in the home, prosperity, wishes

In the Garden:

We don't know about you, but in our gardens they flourish without assistance.

Additional Uses:

Many parts make an excellent diuretic. (Another French name for dandelion is *pis-en-lit*.)

Interesting Fact:

The sap is believed to cure warts.

Dill

Dill spices pickles and is used in salads and a variety of culinary dishes, but its medicinal qualities date back to ancient Egypt, where it was used as a digestive aid. Dill can also be used to increase a mother's milk, stimulate appetite, reduce swelling, and control flatulence in babies and adults.

In the Middle Ages, dill was used to ward off witchcraft. Today, chewing dill wards off bad breath.

Use in Gris Gris Bags for:
Passion, prosperity, protection

In the Garden:
This annual prospers in loose, well-drained soil and full sun.

Additional Uses:
The Greeks believed dill stopped hiccoughs.

Interesting Fact:
Roman soldiers returned home with dill garlands.

Echinacea

Echinacea is primarily used to promote the immune system and to purify the blood. Native Americans used the herb for a variety of ailments, from snake bites to burn and wound treatments.

Also called the coneflower for its conical blossoms, echinacea is used in gris gris bags for prosperity, but may also be added to increase the power of any spell. If used in an abundance bag with other prosperity herbs, for instance, echinacea will increase the power of those herbs.

Use in Gris Gris Bags for:
Prosperity, spell enhancer

In the Garden:
Native to the prairie, echinacea prefers raised beds, alkaline soil, and full sun.

Additional Uses:
Echinacea provides a colorful, fragrant addition to any garden.

Interesting Fact:
Echinacea was a popular anti-infective drug in the late nineteenth and early twentieth centuries. It lost its popularity by 1930.

Fava Beans (See **Mojo Beans**)

Fennel

Ancient Greeks battled the Persians in a field of fennel at Marathon, and it's believed that Greeks and Romans chewed fennel to give them courage in battle. Fennel chewing also decreases appetite, which may have been why soldiers used it before battle.

On Midsummer's Eve, fennel was traditionally hung over doorways for protection; people still use it as a threshold protector. Fennel was also pushed into keyholes to keep out evil spirits. It is one of the Anglo-Saxon nine sacred herbs.

Fennel seeds taste like licorice, much like its relatives dill and anise do, and stories indicate that some Puritans chewed the seeds to help keep their eyes open during long sermons.

Use in Gris Gris Bags for:

Courage, healing, protection, purification, repelling negativity

In the Garden:

Fennel prefers standard or moderately fertile, well-drained soil, in full sun with plenty of moisture.

Additional Uses:

Fennel is an excellent insect repellant, and the seeds are great additives to breads, dips, and sauces and make a good breath freshener.

Interesting Fact:

Fennel is used extensively in the cooking of fish.

Fenugreek

Although this herb, a member of the pea family, was named for its use as Greek cattle fodder, it has been employed for centuries as medicine and in the culinary arts. Evidence of fenugreek use has been found in 4000 B.C. Iraq, ancient Judah, the tomb of Tutankhamun, and the gardens of Charlemagne. The Chinese used fenugreek for digestive and menstrual complaints, and various folk remedies insist it cures diabetes, anemia, ulcers, and rickets, and aids in reducing fevers.

Modern research has found that fenugreek seeds contain up to 30 percent mucilage, which makes it useful as a poultice for inflammation, ulcers, and bruises. As a tea, fenugreek may aid digestive problems. Dr. Robert Atkins believed that pulverized fenugreek seeds reduced blood fat and sugar levels in Type I and II diabetics.[23]

Use in Gris Gris Bags for:
Passion, prosperity

In the Garden:
Cultivate in full sun in fertile, alkaline, well-drained soil.

Additional Uses:
As a culinary herb, fenugreek seed is used in curry powders and chutneys in India.

Interesting Fact:
Fenugreek may be boiled to create a yellow dye.

Ferns

Ferns growing at your doorstep or inside your home serve as protectors. Whether carried or worn, ferns allow the bearer to discover treasure, and carrying the seeds will make you invisible (or so the legends say).

Moonwart, a type of fern, was used to open locks and doors when placed inside the keyhole. Moonwart is also effective in prosperity spells.

Use the leaves or seeds in gris gris bags for a variety of intentions.

Use in Gris Gris Bags for:
Luck, prosperity, protection, rain-making, repelling negativity

---

23. Jack Staub, op. cit.

In the Garden:
Ferns grow in a variety of climates but prefer moist composted soil and shade.

Additional Uses:
Ferns are a sacred plant of midsummer.

Interesting Fact:
When burned outside, it will elicit rain.

Feverfew

The Latin word for feverfew, *febrifugia*, means "driver out of fevers." The Greek physician Dioscorides believed feverfew aided in the contraction of the uterus during labor and the delivery of the afterbirth.

A member of the daisy family, feverfew has been nicknamed "bride's buttons" for its small, daisy-like blooms. Herbalist Nicholas Culpeper claimed it was governed by Venus and therefore associated with women's ailments. Recent studies are showing that eating three to four small feverfew leaves per day is effective in reducing the muscle spasms that produce migraine headaches.

Carrying feverfew has been known to prevent accidents, so add it to your gris gris bag if you're as clumsy as we are.

Use in Gris Gris Bags for:
Preventing accidents, protection, repelling negativity

In the Garden:
A member of the daisy family, feverfew is a hardy plant that prefers well-drained soil in full sun to partial shade.

Additional Uses:
Feverfew is not just for migraines. The herb has been and still is noted for general headache relief.

Interesting Fact:
In the seventeenth century, Gervase Markham used the herb in a lotion to remove freckles.

Five-Leaf Grass or Five-Fingers (See **Cinquefoil**)

Garlic

For thousands of years, cultures across the globe have employed garlic. The ancient Egyptians worshipped the herb, and Olympians used its pungent bulb to enhance strength. Early Jews, Arabs, and Babylonians recorded using garlic as a medicinal herb and in cooking, and the Chinese ate garlic to prevent colds, diarrhea, dysentery, tuberculosis, and other diseases. Spanish explorer Hernando Cortes brought the herb to North America, and later, Native Americans ate garlic for healing purposes.

European peasants wore garlic around their necks to ward off evil, vampires, and the plague and, according to Southern folklore, carrying garlic in your pocket wards off evil. Around the time of World War I, garlic was used to fight infection in wounds and worn to protect against influenza epidemics. Eleanor Roosevelt took garlic pills every day because her doctor said they would improve her memory.

Recent studies have proven garlic's medicinal attributes, most notably to reduce the threat of colds, improve the function of the heart, and kill harmful bacteria.

Use in Gris Gris Bags for:
Endurance, healing, protection, strength

In the Garden:
For harvest in the fall, plant garlic cloves (even the ones you buy in the grocery store) in early spring, even before the last frost. The cloves should be planted in rich, light soil with good drainage, about 2 inches deep and about 6 inches apart, in full sun. Cut flower stalks back in early summer to allow the plant to develop the bulb. If planted near fruit trees, garlic repels moles, and if planted near roses, it repels aphids.

Additional Uses:

The uses of garlic as a medicinal herb are too numerous to mention, from fighting infection and types of fungi and bacteria (such as yeast) to lowering blood pressure, thinning blood, promoting the immune system, and relieving coughs and sore throats. Some studies have linked garlic to curing gastric cancer. As a culinary herb, the pungent flavor adds great taste to many dishes. Nipped bulbs sprinkled with olive oil and pepper are delicious on their own.

Interesting Fact:

The word "garlic" comes from the Old English *gar leac*, meaning "spear leek." The upturned bulb resembles a spear.

Ginger

This "warm" pungent herb helps the circulation of energy, much like cayenne. The Chinese use ginger for colds, flus, and coughs and as a spicy antidote to nausea. North American wild ginger was used by Native Americans as a food flavorer and for spasms of the bowels and stomach, and as a stimulant against colds.

Since ginger produces heat within the body when eaten, it can be used to fire up a love spell or ignite money and success in a venture. To invoke a wish, place ginger root along with other wishful herbs in a gris gris bag, hold the bag in your palm, and visualize your wish. Another way to use ginger root is to write your wish upon its skin before placing in the bag. (Some spells suggest throwing the root in water with the wish upon it.)

Use in Gris Gris Bags for:

Health, love, passion, prosperity, wishes

In the Garden:

Grow ginger in warm climates in moist, well-drained soil and partial shade.

Additional Uses:

Ginger compresses or baths have been used for arthritis, gout, backaches, and headaches, plus relieving menstrual cramps.

Interesting Fact:

Ginger originated in China, where it is still used extensively in cuisine. Americans, however, prefer the herb in baked goods such as gingerbread, gingerbread cookies, and pumpkin pie.

Ginseng

Ginseng is one of the oldest cultivated herbs, and has long been valued by the Chinese as a cure-all. For more than two thousand years, it has been used in Oriental medicine to treat anemia and heart problems or promote longevity and cure impotency. Because the shape of the ginseng root resembles a human body, people once believed that it could cure all human ailments.

One legend says that specific hunters were used to gather ginseng. They traveled at night with bows and arrows. The ginseng glowed, according to the story, which was helpful since it also moved around; the glow enabled the hunters to keep it in their sights. Amazingly, an American researcher at the USDA Economic Botany Laboratory, who planted ginseng, found that the herb had shifted in the garden.[24]

There are two types of ginseng: American and Chinese. Native Americans used the herb medicinally, but were not quite as excited about ginseng as their Chinese brethren. Nevertheless, they used ginseng for colds, coughs, impotency, infertility, and fevers.

Use in Gris Gris Bags for:

Fertility, healing, love, passion, repelling negativity, wishes

In the Garden:

Ginseng prefers rich, well-drained soil in cool shade.

---

24. Gaea and Shandor Weiss, op cit.

Additional Uses:
Some cultures used ginseng as an aphrodisiac.

Interesting Fact:
Ginseng has been found effective for motion sickness.

Hyssop

Hyssop is probably one of the most-mentioned herbs in the Bible, repeatedly referred to as a symbol of cleansing and purification. In Psalms 51:7, after bedding Bathsheba, the wife of Uriah, David says, "Purge me with hyssop and I shall be clean." Leviticus advises using hyssop to clean a leper's home, and in John 19:29, when Christ cried out with thirst, soldiers "put a sponge full of the sour wine on a hyssop branch and held it to his mouth." The name may derive from the Greek *hussopos* and the Hebrew *ezob*, meaning "holy herb," for it was used by both ancient cultures to purify temples.

Hyssop has a camphorous scent and serves as a fumigant, which may be why it was strewn over floors where disease was present. Penicillin mold grows on its leaves, which is possibly another reason ancient peoples considered it a purifying herb.

Hyssop was also thought to drive away evil; a gathering of hyssop was used like a broom to sweep away negativity.

Use in Gris Gris Bags for:
Healing, protection, purification, repelling negativity

In the Garden:
Hyssop demands full sun and well-drained soil.

Additional Uses:
An infusion of hyssop leaves and flower tops makes an excellent expectorant.

Interesting Fact:
Hyssop oil is used in liquors such as Benedictine and Chartreuse.

Ivy

This lovely climbing plant that stands guardian flourishes in many climates, conditions, and soils, which may be one reason why it's associated with luck and tenacity in love. Ivy was used to crown brides and grooms in wedding ceremonies before Christians banned the practice as too pagan.

Twigs of ivy were used in salves to treat sunburn and in poultices for ulcers, boils, and abscesses. The ancient Greeks thought ivy prevented intoxication and Bacchus, the god of wine, had a thyrsus crowned with ivy. The Celtic Tree Alphabet name for ivy is *Gort*.

Use in Gris Gris Bags for:
Love, luck, marriage, protection

In the Garden:
Ivy grows well in various conditions; plant it next to something it can climb.

Additional Uses:
In England, it was believed that drinking from an ivy cup would cure a child of whooping cough.

Interesting Fact:
One legend has it that if a man places under his pillow one of ten leaves gathered on October 31, he will dream of his future bride. For women, there is this ditty: *"Ivy, ivy, I love you, In my bosom I put you, The first young man who speaks to me, My future husband he shall be."*

Job's Tears

Many people string the seeds of this annual grass into prayer beads for protection and healing; the seeds have a natural opening, making them a perfect bead from nature. Because the seeds resemble tears, they are associated with Job of the Old Testament, a man who endured great suffering. The plant has also been called David's tears and Christ's tears.

Some necklaces made of Job's tears are given to sick people to assist in their recovery. Job's tears seeds may be carried for luck as well.

Use in Gris Gris Bags for:
Healing, luck, protection

In the Garden:
Plant in sun to partial shade, in warm climates or indoors, and water regularly. Job's tears do not tolerate frost and cold.

Additional Uses:
Job's tears seeds are edible—they can be roasted or boiled like rice or milled into flour. In India, elephants are quite fond of the leaves.

Interesting Fact:
Both the Indians and Japanese use Job's tears to make beer.

Lavender

Lavender has been used over the centuries in sachets, baths, soaps, and perfumes and is closely identified with love. Aromatherapy experts can easily describe the power of the herb's aroma, which is highly relaxing; it provides stress relief and cures for headaches. Lavender is used in baths and placed on pillows to induce sleep. And, of course, lavender has a reputation for inciting the aphrodisiacal feelings of love.

The medicinal applications of lavender focus on dispelling headaches, but lavender has also been recommended for menstrual problems, sore throats, repelling insects, curing insect bites, and purifying wounds. In 1653, the herbalist Nicholas Culpeper cited lavender for "the tremblings and passions of the heart, and faintings and swoonings." The Chinese used lavender oil in a cure-all oil called White Flower Oil.

Overall, lavender is best known for its scent. It's used in linen closets to freshen sheets and pillowcases, made into "wands" for closets and drawers, and dried in potpourris to provide fresh scent throughout the house. Tea houses commonly use lavender in teas (which may relieve nervous conditions), and bed-and-breakfasts place sprigs of lavender on their guests' pillows for sweet dreams.

Use in Gris Gris Bags for:
Good marriage, happiness, love, peace, purification, sweet dreams

In the Garden:
The most common varieties of lavender are English lavender, which is the most aromatic, and French lavender, which prefers a well-drained soil and sunny environment such as that found near the Mediterranean. Lavender doesn't like cold, wet, or windy climates, but may be moved to a greenhouse in winter in northern areas. A couple of ideal spots for lavender in the U.S. include the hill country of Texas and parts of California.

Additional Uses:
Lavender oil has been reported to repel insects on both humans and pets. The herb has also been noted to protect women against abusive husbands.

Interesting Fact:
In France, children bathe in lavender to maintain good health, and lavender is hung in room corners to repel mosquitoes.

Lemon Verbena

Native to South and Central America, lemon verbena was obtained by the Spanish conquistadors and brought to Spain in the seventeenth century. It was named for Maria Luisa, wife to King Charles IV. One of its names, *aloysia triphylla*, refers to both Luisa (*aloysia*) and the plant's three leaves (*triphylla*).

Lemon verbena is often confused with vervain (*Verbena officinalis*), since it also goes by the name *verveine odorante*. It is used as a fever reducer, sedative, digestive aid, and in aromatherapy.

Use in Gris Gris Bags for:
Love, purification, strength

In the Garden:
Plant in full sun in moist soil, in climates free from frost.

Additional Uses:
Lemon verbena leaves smell like lemon when crushed, so they make a nice tea or additives to meats and stuffing.

Interesting Fact:
The dried leaves of lemon verbena retain their scent for up to three years.

Marjoram

Marjoram comes in two varieties—wild and sweet—with wild marjoram (*origanum*) called "oregano." But whatever name it goes by, marjoram is a fragrant herb. It is habitually grown in gardens to ward off evil, and used in bags within closets to ward off moths.

Ancient Greeks and Romans used marjoram at weddings, and the Roman goddess Juno, protector of women, wore a marjoram crown.

Marjoram was also placed on tombs and grown at gravesites, in the belief that if the herb survived, the dead would be at peace.

Use in Gris Gris Bags for:
Happiness, healing, love, marriage, protection, repelling negativity

In the Garden:
This hardy perennial prefers a sunny climate with dry, light soil.

Additional Uses:
Sweet marjoram with its delightful fragrance was one of the many stewing herbs used to freshen homes.

Interesting Fact:
Marjoram is derived from the Greek for "joy of the mountain."

Mint

What's a garden without the refreshing scent of mint, or a summer's day without a cool glass of mint iced tea?

One of the oldest recorded herbs, mint was found in Egyptian tombs as far back as 1000 B.C. Aristotle found mint to be a powerful aphrodisiac, and the Anglo-Saxons used several types of mint in salves they believed cured just about everything.

In Greek mythology, Hades of the Underworld loved the nymph Minthe, so Hades' jealous wife turned her into an herb. In *One Thousand and One Nights*, young Scheherazade, who tells stories to King Shahryar every night in order to stay alive, refreshes herself every morning with mint tea.

Use in Gris Gris Bags for:
Happiness, prosperity

In the Garden:
Mint grows well in most gardens, preferring moist, rich soil and some shade.

Additional Uses:
A great culinary herb, mint also settles stomach distress.

Interesting Fact:
If mint blooms on St. John's Day (June 24), the finder will receive everlasting happiness.

Mistletoe

Most people think of mistletoe as the plant to kiss beneath at Yule, but this herb, which grows as a parasite upon its host, has a long history of magical associations.

The Druids considered mistletoe sacred, second only to the mighty oak and especially if found growing on an oak. Pliny the Elder reported that Druid priests and priestesses revered mistletoe for its healing properties, and would cut it from the oak with a golden sickle in their rites. The plant was also thought to aid barren animals, and many European cultures used mistletoe for fertility treatments and as an antidote to poison. Other traditions include hanging mistletoe in the bedroom for sweet and prophetic dreams or using it as protection against all kinds of accidents, such as lightning and fires.

Mistletoe is an unusual plant, budding in May with flowers that do not open until February. The fruit takes up to two years to develop. Mistletoe also germinates only in light, whereas most plants require darkness. Even its name shows its uniqueness: from the Anglo-Saxon *mistl*, meaning "different," and *tan*, meaning "twig."

Use in Gris Gris Bags for:
Fertility, healing, love, prophetic dreams, protection, protection from accidents, repelling negativity, sweet dreams

In the Garden:
Mistletoe is a parasite and can be found growing on trees in many climates.

Additional Uses:
Place in a dream pillow for restful sleep, peaceful dreams, and enhanced fertility.

Interesting Fact:
Mistletoe is sometimes worn for luck in hunting.

Mojo Beans (Fava Beans)

Every March since the Middle Ages, Sicilians have decorated church altars to pay homage to St. Joseph, the patron saint of workers, for protecting them from famine. The tradition continues in New Orleans, where a large Sicilian population celebrates St. Joseph's Day, March 19, with elaborate altars of wreaths, crosses, and of course food. Among the food items are dried mojo (fava) beans, a crop once used for cattle fodder but believed to have carried Sicilians through one of the island's worst famines.

Sicilians often carry these beans in their pockets for luck and good fortune, and some place the beans in pantries to ensure that no one in the household will experience hunger. Favas are also called mojo beans and African wishing beans, and are used for wishes and to ensure good fortune.

Use in Gris Gris Bags for:
Luck, overcoming difficulties, prosperity

In the Garden:
Plant in full sun in average, well-drained, but moist soil.

Additional Uses:
Fava may be a natural alternative to Viagra.

Interesting Fact:
Fava is a hardy plant that's easy to grow and harvest.

Moss

Moss is a tenacious plant, surviving in odd places and deriving its magical properties from its host tree. It absorbs water through its leaves and requires little maintenance. According to Mrs. Grieve in *A Modern Herbal*, "Every part of the [sphagnum] moss is permeated with minute tubes and spaces, resulting in a system of delicate capillary tubes, having the effect of a very fine sponge. The cells readily absorb water and retain it. The water can be squeezed out, but the moss does not collapse and is ready to take in fluid again."

Native Americans used sphagnum moss as diapers. Dried pieces of Irish moss, found in coastal areas, can be boiled down and used to soothe sore throats.

Taken from gravestones, moss is believed to bring good financial luck.

Use in Gris Gris Bags for:
Luck, prosperity

In the Garden:
Moss prefers humid, shady areas.

Additional Uses:
Use moss to stuff poppets or voodoo dolls.

Interesting Fact:
Sphagnum moss has been used as a dressing for wounds.

Mugwort (Wormwood, Southernwood)

Mugwort is part of the genus *Artemisia*, which also contains worm-wood and southernwood. Its Latin name, *Artemisia Vulgaris*, may have come from the Greek moon goddess Artemis, or else the queen of Halicarnassus, Artemisia, who created a tomb for her husband that became one of the seven wonders of the world.

Mugwort, derived from the Old English *moughte*, meaning "moth" and *wort*, meaning "herbal plant," has been used as a protection herb, to induce prophetic dreams from within dream sachets, and to repel evil. A tea made from mugwort is used to cleanse magical instruments like crystal balls and scrying mirrors, and to aid in reaching the astral plane and out-of-body experiences.

St. John the Baptist was thought to have worn a girdle of mugwort when he entered the wilderness, so the herb is now associated with protecting travelers. Pliny the Elder praised its use for keeping travelers safe.

In Japan, the scent of mugwort was used to exorcise spirits of disease, and in China, mugwort is hung over doorways to keep evil out of the home. Mugwort was also sacred to the Druids, and one of the nine sacred herbs of the *Lacnunga*.

Carried about in a bag, mugwort will attract passion and promote fertility and healing.

Use in Gris Gris Bags for:
Healing, protection, prophetic dreams, psychic powers, repelling negativity, safe travel

In the Garden:
Plant in full sun or light shade in moist soil.

Additional Uses:
Mugwort makes for an effective insect repellant.

Interesting Fact:
Mugwort tea has been used to combat premenstrual syndrome.

Myrtle

This shrub that stays green and "alive" all year makes for strong love-spell bags, as it helps to both attract love and keep it everlasting.

In Greek legend, Myrrha, a favorite priestess of Aphrodite, was sought after by a suitor, so Aphrodite changed her into an evergreen. As myrtle represents love, it was planted around temples dedicated to Aphrodite and woven into bridal bouquets. Romans too used myrtle, as decorations at feasts, celebrations, and weddings.

Myrtle is used to promote fertility, but when used in bridal bouquets it is intended to prevent the bride from becoming pregnant too soon. Planting myrtle on both sides of the house will promote love and peace within, and carrying myrtle wood will give the wearer a youthful appearance.

Use in Gris Gris Bags for:
Fertility, love, peace, prosperity, youth

In the Garden:
Wax and crepe myrtles prefer sun to part shade, in most soils, mostly in Southern and southeastern climates. Crepe myrtles especially enjoy more temperate zones.

Additional use:
Myrtle branches are good for making wreaths and wands.

Interesting Fact:
Shakespeare said that Venus and Adonis should meet under myrtle shade.

Nettle

Nettles are often thought of merely as the annoying plants by the river that produce red welts when brushed against. Stinging nettles, however, are good for clearing the complexion, for making hair lotions that stimulate growth, as an expectorant, at fighting asthma, and, ironically, for relieving snake bites and insect stings. Nettles are also delicious if steamed, and are high in iron and other vitamins and minerals; Milarepa, a Tibetan yogi, lived solely on nettles for years, which turned his skin green. It is one of the nine sacred herbs.

Use in Gris Gris Bags for:

Healing, passion, protection, repelling negativity

In the Garden:

Nettles are found in the wild, but if you'd like to grow your own, they prefer moist areas.

Additional Uses:

In Scotland, nettles are made into soap.

Interesting Fact:

Native Americans used nettles as a diuretic for pregnant women and to help produce smaller, healthier babies.

Oregano (See **Marjoram**)

Parsley

Parsley was a darling among the ancient Greeks, who used it to crown winners of the Isthmian Games. The Greeks also associated the herb with King Archemorus, the forerunner of death, decorating tombs of the dead with parsley and referring to those who were deadly ill with the expression, "to need only parsley." Following in this deadly vein was Hippocrates, who thought virgins who planted parsley might be impregnated by the devil.

Romans preferred their parsley on a plate, both to eat and to ward off contamination. They also hung garlands of parsley at banquets, or wore the herb to counter body odors and fight intoxication.

Parsley is said to promote passion in the eater. Used in a bath, it will purify and eliminate misfortune.

Use in Gris Gris Bags for:
Funerals, luck, passion, protection, purification

In the Garden:
Plant deep in rich, moist soil, in full sun or partial shade.

Additional Uses:
Parsley is high in numerous vitamins and minerals, and cleanses the mouth between courses.

Interesting Fact:
The ancient Greeks planted parsley at the edge of herb beds, which birthed the expression "being at the parsley and rue." This means to be at the beginning of an enterprise.

Pennyroyal

There are two different varieties of pennyroyal, European and American, both members of the mint family. Despite their many similar characteristics, American pennyroyal is an annual that grows primarily in the eastern section of the country, as far south as Florida and Texas, while the perennial European variety is more ornamental, native to the Near East and Europe, and prefers moister soil.

Native Americans used pennyroyal medicinally for colds, headaches, to soothe the stomach, and to relieve cramping and colic. Some advocated drinking pennyroyal tea while soaking your feet in a hot footbath, then sleeping under several blankets to sweat out the cold or flu.

Pennyroyal has also been used to induce menstruation and force abortions, but excess dosages can prove fatal.

The best use of pennyroyal continues to be as an insect repellant—crush the leaves and apply the oil directly to your skin. Many commercial insect repellants name pennyroyal in their list of ingredients. Pregnant women should avoid using pennyroyal, as insect repellant or as anything else.

Use in Gris Gris Bags for:
Good marriage, hearth and home, peace, protection, repelling negativity

In the Garden:
American pennyroyal prefers an acidic, dry soil and full sun. European pennyroyal should be planted in rich, moist soil with full sun to partial shade. European pennyroyal does well in bogs, irrigated fields, and along the edges of water gardens.

Additional Uses:
Pennyroyal works well as a natural flea repellant and should be used in gardens where fleas are a problem. Place fresh leaves in your pet's bed on a regular basis.

Interesting Fact:
The ancient Greeks and Romans used pennyroyal in cooking, and the Greeks often flavored their wine with pennyroyal.

Plantain

A maiden waited by the side of the road for her lover, the legend goes, but she waited so long, she turned into an herb. While plantain is basically a perennial weed that grows wild on roadsides, it has plenty of medicinal and magical uses. The Anglo-Saxons wouldn't have named it one of their nine sacred herbs for nothing.

Crushed plantain leaves alleviate insect bites and stings and stop the itching of poison ivy. Native Americans used the juice for rattlesnake bites (this is one reason why another word for plantain is "snakeweed"). Poultices were used for wounds and rheumatic pain, and some people believe that chewing the root will stop toothache.

In Appalachia, they used plantain seeds as a laxative, and in China, they brewed the herb with flaxseed to restore sexual prowess in men.

Use in Gris Gris Bags for:
Repelling negativity (one of the Anglo-Saxon sacred herbs)

In the Garden:
This hardy plant prospers in average, well-drained soil, in full sun to partial shade.

Additional Uses:
The leaves can be eaten in salads or steamed like spinach.

Interesting Fact:
Native Americans called plantain "white man's foot" because it appeared to grow where the settlers traveled.

Rice

People throw rice at newly married couples to wish them well. This tradition dates back many years, possibly as far back as ancient Egypt, and is thought to represent fertility (rice symbolizing seed) and prosperity (seeds produce a healthy crop).

Use in Gris Gris Bags for:
Fertility, prosperity

In the Garden:
Most rice today is grown commercially because of the precise conditions required to grow a successful crop. A large portion of the United States' rice production comes from Louisiana.

Additional Uses:
Rice is a wonderful complement to most meals, and Cajuns in Louisiana will tell you it can help stretch a meal in hard times like no other food.

Interesting Fact:
Some believe that throwing rice will lead to rain.

Rosemary

The early Arabs thought rosemary could restore lost memory, and the Greeks massaged its oil into their foreheads to improve memory—which is why the herb is connected with remembrance. It is used at funerals, where visitors throw sprigs onto coffins being lowered into the ground.

When placed at the threshold, rosemary is said to protect the home, and it also may be hung over a doorway in a bag to protect all who enter. Burning rosemary cleanses a room of negativity.

This fragrant herb with its blue flowers is also associated with weddings and used in bouquets. It can be placed under the pillow with silver coins, in a dream sachet, to encourage dreams of a future lover. Placed under the pillow without the coins, it wards off evil spirits.

Rosemary is also a symbol of Mary and the Nativity of Christ, and is said to be a strong feminine protection herb. It thrives in coastal areas—its botanical name, *Rosmarinus*, means "dew of the sea."

Use in Gris Gris Bags for:

Love, marriage, passion, purification, remembrance, repelling negativity

In the Garden:

Rosemary prefers sunny, well-drained soil, preferably alkaline, in warm climates. In ideal conditions, rosemary may grow to be quite large, so be sure to give it space.

Additional Uses:

Crushed or minced rosemary leaves enhance poultry, meats, fish, and vegetables and can be used in dressings and marinades.

Interesting Fact:

If a rosemary bush grows big and strong, it signifies that a woman is the head of the household.

Rue

This evergreen shrub is native to southern Europe. Its lovely yellow flowers appear in June and remain bright all summer. Both Leonardo da Vinci and Michelangelo used rue, believing it to enhance their creativity and bring them inner vision. Branches of rue were used to sprinkle holy water during High Mass, and the herb was also employed to ward off plague. The Greeks used it as an anti-poison antidote.

Use in Gris Gris Bags for:
Creativity, health, love, purification, repelling negativity

In the Garden:
Plant in full sun with some shade, in well-drained, alkaline soil.

Additional Uses:
The leaves of rue can remove bruises.

Interesting Fact:
Rue was the inspiration for the suit of clubs in playing cards.

Saffron

Cave paintings found in present-day Iraq show saffron-based pigments fifty thousand years old. Cleopatra bathed in this fragrant herb to become more desirable to men, and the ancient Greeks and Romans used saffron as a perfume. Buddhist priests used it to dye their robes a deep yellow. From the fourteenth to the eighteenth centuries, saffron was used medicinally and as a spice throughout Europe.

Saffron's pungent spice can be used to flavor all kinds of foods, from rice to meat and fish dishes, as well as used in liqueurs to stimulate the appetite. Unfortunately, saffron cannot be grown in the garden for this purpose; it takes seventy-five thousand flowers to produce one pound of the spice.

Use in Gris Gris Bags for:
Happiness, healing, love, passion, psychic powers, strength

In the Garden:
Plant in rich, well-drained soil in sunny, sheltered spots.

Additional Uses:
Herbalist Nicholas Culpeper believed saffron refreshed the spirit, aided the stomach, and cleansed the lungs.

Interesting Fact:
Saffron was once considered an aphrodisiac.

Sage

This versatile herb represents wisdom above all, which is why we call wise men and women "sages." The Greeks believed that those who ate sage would become immortal in wisdom and in years. At one time, elderly women carried a posy of chamomile and sage to represent their wisdom.

The Romans considered sage a sacred herb, believing it to restore memory, and only those in white tunics and clean bare feet could harvest sage, using bronze or silver tools. Before the sage harvest, sacrifices of food and wine were made.

There is an old French proverb that says, "Sage helps the nerves and by its powerful might, palsy is cured and fever put to flight." Sage makes for an excellent antioxidant, anti-inflammatory, and antiseptic, and was used to treat colds, fevers, cholera, and the plague. Its seeds were used in poultices to reduce swelling.

Sage is also planted on graves for remembrance. And if you write a wish on a sage leaf and sleep on it for three nights, you will dream of your wish and then it will come true.

Use in Gris Gris Bags for:
Healing, longevity, prosperity, protection, purification, remembrance, repelling negativity, wisdom, wishes

In the Garden:
Plant in full sun in well-drained soil.

Additional Uses:
A sage-and-vinegar compress can help relieve the pain of bruises.

Interesting Fact:
May seems to be sage's month. In Crete, sage was gathered on the first or second day of May before the sun rises. There is also a saying that associates sage with long life: "He that would live for aye, must eat sage in May."

Sainfoin

Sainfoin is sometimes thought to be the legendary *atterlothe*, one of the nine sacred herbs of the *Lacnunga*, an Anglo-Saxon herbal text. This nutritious plant, found in grasslands and farms throughout Europe, is used to feed horses and cattle—hence its name, *sain foin*, Old French for "healthy hay."

Use in Gris Gris Bags for:
Repelling negativity

In the Garden:
Sanfoin grows in dry, well-drained soil.

Additional Uses:
Sainfoin provides a good nectar source for British honey bees.

Interesting Fact:
Some of the herb's nicknames are "esparcet" and "holy clover."

St. John's Wort

The Scots used this Druid sacred herb as a charm against fairies, and residents of the British Isles hung it over doorways at midsummer to repel negativity. If a person gathered and wore St. John's wort either on midsummer or on a Friday, they were thought to be protected from mental illness.

Christians named this herb for St. John the Baptist, because it is said to bloom on his birthday (June 24). If you pinch its yellow flowers, the petals turn red; some people believed that the herb bleeds red on the day in August when John the Baptist was beheaded.

If St. John's wort is placed under the pillow in a dream sachet, single women will dream of their future husbands. The herb also wards off fevers and cold and is thought to cure depression.

Use in Gris Gris Bags for:
Divination, healing, love, protection against lightning, repelling negativity, strength

In the Garden:
This hardy perennial likes average to poor soil, in full sun to partial shade.

Additional Uses:
Burn St. John's wort to clear the air of negativity.

Interesting Fact:
This versatile herb is used as a resin, tannin, dye, and antidepressant, plus it soothes the digestive system and works as a pain killer and sedative.

Sunflower

The mighty sunflower bursts from the ground every spring. Its massive flower follows the sun as it moves across the sky, then faces east again to catch the first rays of the dawn of the new day. It is not surprising that this incredibly bright flower was used in the religious ceremonies of the Incas and the Aztecs; the priestesses would wear sunflower crowns upon their heads.

The sunflower produces an enormous number of seeds within its intricate geometric pattern. Legends claim that planting sunflowers in your garden and/or eating the seeds will bring good luck. To visualize the truth of a matter, place sunflower seeds or petals beneath your pillow in a dream sachet. Due to its massive seed production, the sunflower also symbolizes fertility.

Use in Gris Gris Bags for:
Fertility, luck, protection, wishes

In the Garden:
Plant in well-drained soil, in full sun. Be sure not to plant sunflowers too close to each other—they need plenty of space to grow individually.

Additional Uses:
All parts of the sunflower are usable, but the seeds are especially healthy, containing 25 percent protein and lots of vitamins and minerals.

Interesting Fact:
Spaniards brought the sunflower back to Europe, but it took a while for the plant to catch on. In Russia, however, sunflowers are quite popular.

Thyme

The Anglo-Saxons used this sweet-smelling herb in their Nine Herb Charm, and Culpeper advised employing thyme as a remedy for nightmares. Fairies and elves were known to adore the herb, which is also extremely popular with bees.

The Egyptians used thyme as an ingredient in embalming fluids for mummifications. The Greeks enlisted thyme to purify coffins, to assure the dead a safe passage into the afterlife. Burned, thyme acts as a purifier and a fumigant against disease and illnesses.

Thyme has long been associated with courage. The Greeks saw thyme as an aid in acting bravely, Roman soldiers bathed with thyme before battle, and English women of the Middle Ages gave knights tokens of thyme before sending them off to war. During the English War of the Roses, English women gave soldiers embroidered renditions of thyme with a bee hovering over it.

During the French Revolution, if a person received a sprig of thyme, it meant they were summoned to a republican meeting. And in

World War I, thymol, an extraction of thyme oil with antiseptic values, was used for treating wounds and purifying the air of hospitals.

Use in Gris Gris Bags for:
Courage, funerals, psychic powers, purification, repelling negativity, sweet dreams

In the Garden:
Plant in full sun in a warm climate, in well-drained lime soil. Creeping varieties of thyme make a great substitute for lawns. A delightful aroma arises when the herb is walked upon and you don't have to mow it (thus not polluting the environment).

Additional Uses:
Thyme is a wonderful antioxidant and antimicrobial and owns flavanoids and a variety of minerals.

Interesting Fact:
Some believe that Jesus' cradle in Bethlehem was lined with thyme.

Valerian

Valerian is a natural tranquilizer, which is why it may be associated with spells for sweet dreams. Some believe the Pied Piper used valerian to drug the cats and rats he lured out of town. If you plant valerian in your garden, your cat will love you forever.

Valerian isn't used in American prescriptions, but you can find it in European pharmaceuticals. However, anyone can make a calming tea by brewing 1 teaspoon of the fresh root in 1 pint of water. Drink cold and use only in small doses.

The Native Americans used valerian as a cure for swollen joints.

Use in Gris Gris Bags for:
Love, protection, purification, sweet dreams

In the Garden:
Plant in rich moist soil, in full sun to partial shade.

Additional Uses:
Valerian was once used to treat the plague and epilepsy.

Interesting Fact:
Ancients used valerian as a perfume, but some people claim it smells like dirty socks.

Vervain

With nicknames like "herb of enchantment" and "holy herb," you know that vervain is a magical plant. It was used by the Egyptians and was sacred to the Romans, Persians, and Druids, and some Christians believe vervain was placed on Christ's wounds after the crucifixion. Roman priests used vervain to purify temples devoted to Jupiter, and Druid daughters wore vervain as a crown when initiated.

Vervain has many uses. When carried, the legends say, it will bring a person everlasting youth. Placed within a dream sachet beneath your pillow, it will deliver sweet dreams. Blue vervain is planted by doorsteps to attract lovers and is a potent love charm at weddings. Vervain sprinkled about the house with other peaceful herbs will bring about a calm, loving atmosphere.

Use in Gris Gris Bags for:
Happiness, love, peace, prosperity, protection, protection against lightning, purification, sweet dreams, youth

In the Garden:
Plant in rich, moist loam, in full sun.

Additional Uses:
Herbalist Nicholas Culpeper said this about vervain: "Used with lard it helps pain in secret parts."

Interesting Fact:
In medieval times, vervain was recommended for removing pimples: stand outside, place vervain in a handkerchief, and rub it over the

pimple when you see a shooting star fly by. If you use your bare hands, the pimple will rub off into your hand, so keep the handkerchief handy.

Watercress

For centuries, people have sung the praises of watercress, one of the Anglo-Saxon nine sacred herbs. Dioscorides claimed it was a wonderful medicinal plant, supporting the Greek proverb that one should "eat cress, and learn more wit." Francis Bacon wrote that the "eating of watercress doth restore the wanted bloom to the cheeks of old-young ladies."

Watercress is full of vitamins and minerals. It's also a blood purifier, tonic, and digestive aid, and stimulates the appetite.

Use in Gris Gris Bags for:
Repelling negativity

In the Garden:
As a wild plant that prefers moist areas, such as ditches, watercress can be grown in the garden under similarly wet conditions.

Additional Uses:
To make a traditional watercress sandwich, butter the bread and season it with pepper or lemon juice, then top it with a sprig of watercress. More modern recipes blend watercress with cream cheese and other ingredients in a food processor, then spread it on the bread.

Interesting Fact:
Eaten fresh, watercress has a peppery taste. Thus its nicknames, "poor man's pepper" and "peppergrass."

Wolfbane (See Aconite)

Yarrow

The Druids used yarrow for weather forecasting, and the Chinese turned to it to forecast their futures. The Romans named the herb after Achilles' spear, which could both kill and heal, and utilized its medicinal properties on the battlefield. The Anglo-Saxon word for yarrow, *gearwe*, means "repairer of bodies."

Yarrow was assigned to St. John the Baptist and hung on St. John's Eve (June 23) for protection against evil and sickness. Many thought that witches used yarrow in spells, which is why other names for the herb include "devil's plaything" and "devil's nettle." Nevertheless, branches were hung over newborn cradles to protect babies from witches and fairies.

Yarrow is also associated with love, and used in wedding bouquets called "seven years' love." Brides who carry yarrow are assured of at least seven years of successful marriage.

Place an ounce of yarrow in a flannel bag and put it under the pillow. Repeat these words to see a future mate:

> *Thou pretty herb of Venus' tree,*
> *Thy true name it is Yarrow;*
> *Now who my bosom friend must be,*
> *Pray tell thou me to-morrow.* [25]

Use in Gris Gris Bags for:
Courage, love, luck, protection, repelling negativity

Additional Uses:
If a woman picks yarrow off the grave of a young man during a full moon, she will dream of her future lover.

Interesting Fact:
The Irish believed that yarrow was the first herb that Jesus picked.

---

25. James Orchard Halliwell, *Popular Rhymes and Nursery Tales* (London: John Russell Smith, 1849).

ROOTS

· · · · · · · · · · · · · · ·

Roots have historically been vital ingredients in mojo or gris gris bags. In fact, because so many people incorporated roots into their spells, pouches were often called "root bags." Conjurers advertising their wares sometimes referred to themselves as "root doctors."

Many of the roots associated with spells resemble the intention of the spell—lucky hand root, which mimics a human hand, is used in spells to attract luck (especially when gambling). Other roots, such as High John the Conqueror, are associated with courageous tales, giving them power through story.

Angelica Root

The Latin name for angelica root, *Angelica archangelica*, was thought to be a reference to the feast day of Archangel Michael. Michaelmas occurs on September 29, when the plant would burst into bloom. Another explanation for the name is that an angel revealed the plant, in a dream, as a cure for the plague.

Northern Europeans found that angelica root's leaves, seeds, and root were a cure-all for a variety of ailments, but also believed the entire plant could ward off evil spells. Because of this power, the plant was labeled "the root of the Holy Ghost."

The sixteenth-century poet Guillaume du Bartas wrote,

> *Angelica, that happy counterbane*
> *sent down from Heav'n by some celestial scout*
> *as well the name and nature both avowt.*

Use in Gris Gris Bags for:
Prosperity, protection, repelling negativity

In the Garden:
Enjoys damp, rich soil, preferably near running water. Dig up the roots in the fall and dry immediately.

Additional Uses:
Angelica used in various spells is said to repel negativity and curses.

Interesting Fact:
Angelica is used as a flavoring in beverages and liqueurs.

Devil's Shoestring

This root, which resembles a shoestring, is commonly carried in the pocket as a mojo to bring about a new job or luck at the gaming tables (and prosperity in general), and also to protect the carrier from harm. Some of the plants known as devil's shoestring include hobblebush, cramp bark (for its reference to alleviating menstrual cramps), and black haw.

In the voodoo tradition, spells call for using nine strings of this root. You can also use devil's shoestring to tie a bag nine times.

Use in Gris Gris Bags for:
Employment, gaming luck, protection, repelling negativity

In the Garden:
Devil's shoestring grows wild in woods.

Additional Uses:
Devil's shoestring can aid in receiving raises and promotions

Interesting Fact:
As part of the honeysuckle family of North America, devil's shoestring can be any of several species of viburnum.

High John the Conqueror

High John the Conqueror root (or "John the Conqueroo") was named after a folk hero of this name, an African prince who ended up a slave in America. Despite his predicament, High John evaded his masters through trickery. This made his tale especially powerful for African slaves, particularly those in New Orleans, as they reveled in a slave who kept his spirits up and broke free.

In the novel *Their Eyes Were Watching God*, Zora Neale Hurston writes that High John returned to Africa but "he left his power here, and placed his American dwelling in the root of a certain plant. Only possess that root, and he can be summoned at any time."

High John the Conqueror is the top dog in the voodoo herbal hierarchy, able to ward off any disease or ill wind. Legend has it that carrying the root will bring a person luck, winnings in gambling, and sexual prowess. There are numerous blues songs that mention High John the Conqueror, such as Muddy Waters' rendition of Willie Dixon's "(I'm Your) Hoochie Coochie Man" in 1954.

Use in Gris Gris Bags for:
Gambling, luck, prosperity, protection

In the Garden:
High John the Conqueror, which has a vine above ground, is a member of the honeysuckle family and a cousin of the sweet potato.

Additional Uses:
Don't ingest this plant, for it's a strong laxative.

Interesting Fact:
There is also a root called Low John the Conqueror, whose attributes are health, passion, and protection.

Lucky Hand Root

Certain species of orchids create a root shaped like a hand. Called "lucky hand," this root will bring good luck and money to gamblers who carry it, either in their pocket or within a bag.

Use in Gris Gris Bags for:
Employment, gambling, luck, prosperity, protection

In the Garden:
Lucky hand root enjoys Southern climates.

Additional Uses:

Musicians use this root to assist in their performances, believing that the fingers of the root can assist their own.

Interesting Fact:

Also known as "helping hand."

Mandrake

Because its shape resembles a human body, mandrake was often used as a poppet as well as in numerous spells and gris gris bags. For instance, many people hang mandrake on a mantel to protect the home and attract happiness and prosperity. Placed above the head of the bed, mandrake protects the sleeper and induces a healthy sleep; the ancient Greeks, Egyptians, and Arabs swore by this.

Mandrake contains chemicals that are trance-inducing, which is why the plant appears in numerous Egyptian artworks along with water lilies and poppies (opium). In King Tutankhamun's tomb, for example, a chest was found with art that showed him failing in health while his wife offered him blue water lilies and poppies, and two servants picked mandrake fruits. Tutankhamun's jewelry had mandrakes as well.

Pliny the Elder suggested drinking mandrake juice before operations, claiming the smell put patients to sleep. The Greek surgeon Dioscorides used mandrake to cure insomnia, as well to ease pain in surgery.

Some believe a mandrake root must be "activated." To do so, leave the root to air for three days, then soak it in warm water overnight.

Carrying mandrake attracts love and wards off illness. Placing mandrake inside a bag, next to a silver coin, is thought to increase a prosperity spell. It is rumored that saying four Masses over the root and then placing it inside a black silk bag ensures safe travel.

Use in Gris Gris Bags for:

Fertility, healing, love, prosperity, protection, repelling negativity, safe travel, sweet dreams

In the Garden:
Mandrake prefers warm climates.

Additional Uses:
In small doses, mandrake root is known to stimulate glands.

Interesting Fact:
American mandrake is also called a "May apple." The mandrake's fruit resembles oval, lemon-colored apples, and taste a bit like straw-berries.

FLOWERS
· · · · · · · · · · · · · · · ·

Flowers, like so many aspects of nature, have a mixed reputation. According to superstition, they can be bad omens—it was once believed that white flowers foretold death, and that flowers with drooping heads and heavy scents contained the souls of the departed. Dead flowers were to be left untouched, as they were contaminated with death. But despite these dubious legends, flowers have primarily been considered universally pleasant and, in more recent times, are thought to be signs of protection and glad tidings.

Color symbolism strongly influences the magical role of flowers, and the similarity of the shape of a blossom to a human face makes us feel even more connected to them. It is said that a blooming marigold brings luck with money because of the blossom's resemblance to a coin, while the pansy's heart-shaped petals are a perfect match for intentions involving affairs of the heart.

The beauty of flowers remains unparalleled. They are constant reminders of the wonders of the universal hand that paints so freely, with such an infinite palette. And whether laden with spiny tufts or draped in a velvet cloak, flowers seem to return our gaze. We gather them, grow them, nurture them, and pamper them in hopes that their glorious faces will emerge. When they unfurl their blazing brilliance, they can illuminate a countryside. When worn, they sparkle more radiantly than any jewel. When gathered for a gris gris, they help focus the magical objective with their color, fragrance, and innate purpose.

Camellia

Camellias have long been associated with fortitude because they bloom in the winter months. We live in South Louisiana and Southern California, respectively, ideal climates for these beautiful blossoms to grace us during winter. It's not uncommon for New Orleans residents to place camellia flowers in bowls of water to grace tables decorated for Mardi Gras.

Camellias also represent wealth and abundance. Planting camellias on your property will attract prosperity, as will placing the flowers about the house. Although they are too large to put inside a spell sachet whole, having a camellia in water nearby while creating prosperity bags will increase your call for good fortune.

Use in Gris Gris Bags for:
Endurance, prosperity

In the Garden:
Camellias prefer temperate climates, and most enjoy partial to full shade.

Additional Uses:
The black and green tea that we commonly drink is derived from *Camellia Sinensis* of China and has been produced for more than two thousand years. Green tea is produced from drying the green leaves of the plant, while black tea is the result of fermented *Camellia Sinensis* leaves. Most of the camellias in Southern gardens today are *Camellia Japonica*, *Camellia Sasanqua*, and other hybrids.

Interesting Fact:
There are 2,300 named cultivars registered with the American Camellia Society.

Cowslip (See **Primrose**)

Jasmine
Not only is jasmine hailed for treating depression and acting as an expectorant for coughs, but its lovely, star-shaped white flowers produce a beautiful scent. Jasmine oil is used in soaps, perfumes, and cosmetics, and in food products such as tea and soft drinks.

There are many different types of jasmine, some more fragrant than others. Night-blooming jasmine releases a lovely scent at dusk, and climbing jasmine covers trellises and fences beautifully.

Use in Gris Gris Bags for:
Happiness, love

In the Garden:
Plant in full sun to partial shade, in moist, well-drained soil in warm climates.

Additional Uses:
Jasmine blends well with other oils.

Interesting Fact:
Jasmine is the national flower of several countries.

Lily

The lily has long been associated with women and purity. In Greek mythology, it sprang from the milk of Hera, wife of Zeus; the Romans say the lily sprang from the milk of Juno, Hera's counterpart. Lilies grow in the Holy Land, which may be why painters throughout the centuries show Archangel Gabriel holding a lily when delivering the Annunciation to Mary.

The lily is also one of the oldest recorded plants. It's mentioned in a Sumerian text from five thousand years ago, in a description of a city in Persia that was surrounded by fields of lilies. The town's name, Susa, means "lily." It is believed that the flower was carried by merchants to Greece, Rome, Crete, Egypt, and eventually England, falling off their wagons to bloom where it landed.

A legend states that lilies only grow for a good woman.

Use in Gris Gris Bags for:
Protection, purity, repelling negativity

In the Garden:
Plant lily bulbs in small groups of at least three, in areas that get mostly sun, and in well-drained soil consisting of at least one-third organic matter.

Additional Uses:
Dioscorides used lilies with honey to remove wrinkles.

Interesting Fact:
Lilies are believed to keep ghosts out of a house.

Lotus

In many cultures, the lotus is seen as the mystical, divine symbol of beauty, life, and enlightenment. Because the flower closes at the end of the day and descends into the water, then rises and opens at dawn, the Egyptians linked it to the sun, connecting it with creation and rebirth.

Hindus revere the lotus as well, connecting it to the gods Vishnu (sometimes named "the Lotus-Eyed One") and Brahma, and to the goddesses Lakshmi and Sarasvati. The lotus is pervasive in Indian iconography. Like the Egyptians, Hindus admire how the lotus emerges from water and mud in exquisite beauty; it has been said that in "rising up pure and unsullied from stagnant water, the lotus represents the manifestation of God."[26]

Buddhists associate the lotus with purity, and believe that wherever Gautama Buddha stepped, a lotus flower emerged. The International Baha'i community's New Delhi temple, also known as the Lotus Temple, is shaped like a massive lotus flower.

The seeds and pods of the lotus are used in gris gris bags. Whether carried or placed in the home, they bring blessings and good luck, or can be used as an antidote to a love spell.

Use in Gris Gris Bags for:
Birth and rebirth, clarity, good riddance, psychic powers, purification

In the Garden:
The lotus grows in water, in warm climates.

26.　Eliza Rasiwala, "The Bahá'í House of Worship," http://www.bahaindia.org/temple/ba-hapur.html (accessed September 2010).

Additional Uses:

The lotus has a large dried seed head that looks like the top of a watering can. These seed heads are used in dried flower arrangements.

Interesting Fact:

The lotus root is rich in vitamins and minerals, and various parts of this flower have been used in traditional Asian herbal medicine.

Marigold

This golden flower, associated with the sun's powers, has been used worldwide. Native Americans used it to decorate altars and shrines, and the ancient Greeks wore marigold garlands at weddings. The Hindus view marigolds as representations of life, eternity, and health, and use them in funeral pyres; Shakespeare called marigolds a funeral flower. Anne Boleyn used marigolds along with pansies in a bouquet that she carried to court.

Marigolds have been widely used medicinally as well, for varicose veins, conjunctivitis, and hemorrhoids. They make a great ointment for healing wounds and lacerations and in treating acne, dermatitis, and eczema.

For gris gris bags, use the soft golden petals.

Use in Gris Gris Bags for:

Love, peace, sweet dreams

In the Garden:

Marigolds are easily grown from seed in any type of soil, in full sun to partial shade. They bloom all summer (and in spring in the Deep South).

Additional Uses:

Marigolds are used in perfumes.

Interesting Fact:

Marigold flower extract has been shown to booster the immune system and inhibit the replication of the HIV-1 virus.

Passionflower

The "passion" in passionflower is constantly misconstrued. Rather than referring to romantic love, "passion" comes from the Passion of Christ: the herb's five petals and sepals were thought to represent the ten faithful apostles of Jesus, and its cornea the crown of thorns Christ wore to his crucifixion. Plus, the five stamens represented the five wounds of Christ. According to legend, missionaries spotted this flower growing in South America and saw it as a sign that they would be able to convert the natives.

Passionflower has a slightly narcotic affect and has been used as a sedative, a calming agent, and a cure for insomnia. Place dried flowers in dream pillows for a restful night's sleep, or in a bath to soothe the skin and soul.

When it is placed in bags and kept within the home, it will promote peace. If you carry it on you, you will attract friends.

Use in Gris Gris Bags for:
Friendships, peace, sweet dreams

In the Garden:
Prefers fertile, well-drained soil, in partially shaded areas.

Additional Uses:
Passionflower was thought to lower blood pressure and treat diarrhea and dysentery.

Interesting Fact:
The passionflower, also known as maypop, is the official state wildflower of Tennessee.

Primrose and Cowslip

Primrose and its cousin cowslip are both beautiful flowers that can be gathered in a posey or dried for potpourri. And both are thought to attract fairies.

Carrying primrose in a gris gris bag will attract love; sew its dried leaves and flowers into your children's pillows so that they will always respect you.

Use in Gris Gris Bags for:

Love, protection, psychic powers

In the Garden:

Plant in semi-shade or sun, in moist soil.

Additional Uses:

A tea made from primrose flowers can be used as a sedative or for treating headaches.

Interesting Fact:

Cowslip has a milky scent, which is what gives it its name. You can make cowslip wine or drink the nectar straight from its flowers. The lure of this sweet drink, however, has caused the flower to be picked so frequently that it is nearing extinction.

Roses

It is believed that the cultivation of the rose began about five thousand years ago in China. Ever since, people have adored its fragrance and beauty; no other plant has been more associated with love and passion than roses.

Stories of the rose's romantic power, both mythical and factual, abound throughout history. Cleopatra covered her floor knee-deep in roses in an attempt to seduce Antony (it worked); Confucius loved roses and collected books on the subject; the ancient Greeks believed that roses were the flowers of love, and Romans used rose garlands at banquets, as crowns for bridal couples, and as a source of perfume.

The War of the Roses in fifteenth-century England pitted the House of York and its white rose symbol against the House of Lancaster and its red rose. Shakespeare mentions roses more than fifty times in his writings.

Roses have been used in cooking for centuries. Rosewater is used to create Turkish delight, rose petals make up jams, pies, and salads, and vitamin C-rich rose hips are steeped for teas, wines, and sauces.

The rose is the national floral emblem of the United States. June is National Rose Month.

The best rose buds and petals to use in gris gris bags are those from the most fragrant flowers, such as the old-fashioned roses named "Provence" and "Damask." Most hybrid roses found in nurseries today contain showy, bright-colored blooms but produce little or no smell. It's important for both the bag creator and receiver to inhale the potency of the rose petals and buds within, for the scent evokes images of love and keeps your mind on the task at hand.

Use in Gris Gris Bags for:
Healing (preferably white roses), love, passion, protection (preferably white roses)

In the Garden:
Varieties of roses vary from the small but pungent old-fashioned rose to the always-blooming Knock-Out rose, and conditions vary as well. Most roses bloom in late spring to early summer to fall, depending on the location. If you wish to grow your own roses, contact your local nursery or rose center and ask for varieties that not only smell delicious but flourish in your area. Generally, roses enjoy sunny or lightly shaded spots, and well-drained soil.

Additional Uses:
Roses make excellent potpourri, acting as the basic ingredient in many potpourri mixtures.

Interesting Fact:

Roses were painted on Roman ceilings in rooms where banquets were held. Because diners at these banquets might have a little too much to drink, the expression "*sub rosa*" originated, which meant "under the rose"—in other words, anything said beneath the rose should remain private. Later, roses were hung above meeting places and carved in Christian confessionals. Today, "subrosa" still alludes to secrecy.

TREES

· · · · · · · · · · · · · · · ·

In many ways, trees are like people. Each is an individual, unique to where it originates and where it grows. A tree's face expresses its history, the storms it has weathered, the hardships it's endured, its times of lack and its times of plenty. Trees breathe and have souls, and each type carries with it a purpose. For ages, the purpose of each tree spoke clearly to humanity—the oak was mighty and persevering; the elm was knowing and wise; the maple was sweet and enticing; the eucalyptus was tall and healing; the willow was pliable, gentle, sympathetic, and mournful.

As children, we climbed trees. We sought sanctuary in them, built clubhouses, and were inexplicably drawn to the sticks and twigs that became our companion for the day. Even as adults, we collect leaves and marvel at their shapes and colors, or hold them up to the light and study the veins that run through the diaphanous webbing.

Trees are some of the most magical plants in all existence. They reach out to the sun and drink in the life-giving force that surrounds them. They reach down into the earth and pull what they need, giving back a canopy of shade, tenacity, and clean air. They stand majestic even as seedlings, and hold the mystery of miraculous healing. They can rise from ashes like a phoenix, out of pure persistence, and they speak in a cryptic rustling, weaving sentences with the wind. And yet they still offer up their souls in harvest for their cohabitants on this Earth. They bend as they must with season and with time; they never fear the advent of change, for it defines existence.

Apple

Although in the story of Adam and Eve the apple denotes temptation and sin, in many other contexts throughout history apples symbolize fertility and health, love and prophecy. In ancient Rome, harvest celebrations honored Pomona, the goddess of orchards, seeds, and crops. The apple tree appears in numerous Celtic legends, and as one of the most revered trees of the Druids, it has an Ogham letter—its Celtic Tree Alphabet name is *Quert*. And even our familiar Halloween traditions of hanging apples to catch in mid-air, bobbing for apples, and paring apples were once used to signify who might get married first or the identity of a person's true love.[27]

Today, we claim that "An apple a day keeps the doctor away." There is much truth to that statement, considering apples are good digestives.

Use in Gris Gris Bags for:
Fertility, healing, longevity, love, marriage

Additional Uses:
Rubbing apple slices onto warts is said to make them disappear. Some believe you must bury the slices after using them.

Interesting Fact:
An old Halloween tradition had a woman pare an apple, then toss it over her shoulder. Her true love's first initial was said to be imprinted on the fallen apple.

Ash

Considered a World Tree in many ancient cultures, and a Tree of Life, the ash is associated with water, strength, travel, protection, and balance.

In Norse mythology, Odin hung from ash branches to receive enlightenment about the secrets of the runes. The Norse believed that the ash represented the universe—its roots reached deep into the ground and its branches supported heaven, with the earthly plane balanced in between. Wands and staffs were created out of ash wood, and an ash log makes up the traditional Yule fire burned at the winter solstice. The Celtic Tree Alphabet name for ash is *Nuin*.

Use in Gris Gris Bags for:
Healing, prophetic dreams, prosperity, protection, safe sea travel

27.   Diane C. Arkins, *Halloween: Romantic Art and Customs of Yesteryear* (New Orleans, LA: Pelican Publishing, 2000).

Additional Uses:

Ash has been used for centuries to create tool handles and walking canes, since the protective qualities of the wood are thought to be transferred to the owner.

Interesting Fact:

Sailors carried a cross made out of ash wood to protect them at sea.

Bay Laurel

The ancient Greeks considered the culinary bay laurel tree sacred. The god Apollo was depicted wearing a laurel crown as a celebratory symbol, and the tradition was passed on to the winning Olympians. Since the bay laurel represented glory and greatness, it was also used for crowning outstanding royalty, priests, victorious soldiers, and poets, the latter earning the title of poet laureate.

The bay tree is associated with protective qualities, especially during thunder and lightning; the Roman emperor Tiberius wore laurel crowns during storms. Placing a potted bay laurel at one's front door is said to ward off evil.

Nicholas Culpeper wrote that the bay laurel was "a tree of the Sun, and under the celestial sign Leo, and resisteth witchcraft very potently, as also all the evils old Saturn can do the body of man."[28] In general, bay leaf is considered "a protection and purification herb *par excellence.*"[29]

Bay leaves are also used in many culinary dishes, such as stews, soups. and sauces.

Use in Gris Gris Bags for:

Good fortune, protection, protection against lightning, purification, strength (and victory in athletics)

---

28. *Culpeper's Complete Herbal* (Berkshire, U.K.: Foulsham, 1975).

29. Scott Cunningham, *Cunningham's Encyclopedia of Magical Herbs* (Woodbury, MN: Llewellyn, 2000).

Additional Uses:
Dried bay leaves, mixed with thyme and parsley within a cheese-cloth bag, make up a bouquet garni.

Interesting Fact:
The demise of bay laurel trees is said to be an evil omen. Shakespeare commented in *Richard II*,

> *'Tis thought the king is dead; we will not stay,*
> *The bay trees in our country are all wither'd.*

Birch

In European tradition, the birch tree signifies protection; in Mongolia, shamans used birch as the central pole in yurts; and in Siberia, birch is a symbol of ascent to the other world. Birch also represents new beginnings, as illustrated by its role as the symbol for first moon in the Celts' thirteen-month *Beth-Luis-Nion* calendar. (The *Beth-Luis-Nion* calendar, which is based in the Ogham alphabet, only employs thirteen of the twenty-five Ogham tree symbols; it begins with the winter solstice and tracks the thirteen moons of the lunar year.) Birch's Celtic Tree Alphabet name is *Beith*.

Soft and pliable birch bark is good for a number of things, including broomsticks and as a substitute for paper; the Himalayan birch was used for writing Sanskrit texts. Write a loved one's name on birch bark for spells, and use a birch broom to clear a house of negativity and to invite protection.

Use in Gris Gris Bags for:
Baby blessings, hearth and home, new beginnings, prosperity, protection, protection against lightning

Additional Uses:
Perhaps because birch represents new beginnings and is associated with the Great Mother or Mother Nature, its wood has been used in the creation of cradles.

Interesting Fact:
When a couple "jumped the broom" to get married, the broom was usually made of birch.

Buckeye

The word "buckeye" derives from this tree's fruit, which resembles the eye of a deer (a buck). During the settlement of Ohio, the first tree felled was a buckeye tree; hence, the nicknames "the Buckeye State" and, later, the Ohio State University Buckeyes.

Early travelers to Ohio carried the strange-looking fruit back home in their pockets, saying that the buckeye nut brought them good luck. It's also claimed that the buckeye can relieve rheumatism pain and arthritis.

Use in Gris Gris Bags for:
Luck, protection

Additional Uses:
Buckeye wood can be used for whittling and carving, since it is lighter and softer than other kinds of wood.

Interesting Fact:
The nuts contain tannic acid and are poisonous, but Native Americans would blanch them, extracting the acid and using it to preserve leather.

Cedar

The ancient Greeks considered the cedar tree a good luck tree, and discovered that its branches made fragrant incense. In Sumeria, the cedar is the Tree of Life. Various ancient cultures used cedar in sacrifices, which is why its botanical name is *Thuja*, from the Latin version of the Greek word that meant to fumigate or sacrifice. On the other side of the pond, Native Americans burned the branches in sweat lodges, to induce perspiration and purify the body.

Cedar chips and leaves will repel moths from closets. Clothes chests are made of cedar to protect woolens and other linens against moths; this could be one reason why the tree is associated with purification. Some people burn cedar leaves to purify a home or protect it from harm.

Cedar trees can be found in graveyards, perhaps because cedar, like cypress, was used to build coffins and funeral pyres. Some associate this evergreen tree with protecting the soul from darkness, since cedars will not lose color and die.

Use in Gris Gris Bags for:
Love, prosperity, protection against lightning, purification, repelling negativity

Additional Uses:
A piece of cedar kept in the wallet is thought to attract money.

Interesting Fact:
Many people believe that cedar hung in the home will protect it against lightning strikes.

Cinnamon Tree

Anointing with oil of cinnamon dates back to Biblical times. The ancient Egyptians used cinnamon in their mummy-embalming practices, and cinnamon leaves were draped on Roman temples. The tree is native to Ceylon (now Sri Lanka).

The spice used in cooking is derived from the dried inner bark of the cinnamon tree's branches, and is both fragrant and sweet-spicy in food. It was in high demand for centuries, until other countries learned how to produce it. It is said that the Roman Emperor Nero burned a year's supply of cinnamon (a very expensive undertaking) in penance for killing his wife.

Placing cinnamon in a sachet will attract love and passion, as well as serve as a form of protection.

Use in Gris Gris Bags for:
Love, passion, protection, psychic powers

Additional Uses:
Burning cinnamon bark in the home is said to enhance psychic powers.

Interesting Fact:
It is said that the botanical name *Cinnamomum* derives from *amomon*, from the Hebraic and Arabic term meaning "fragrant spice plant."

Clove Tree

A common presence in the kitchen spice cabinet, cloves are dried flower buds from an evergreen tree native to Indonesia. The name "clove" comes from the French *clou*, which means nail, reflecting the shape of the clove.

As well as adding spice to a meal, cloves are used as breath fresheners and digestion aids, and also to treat toothaches (although applying clove oil to a toothache should be done in moderation). Clove oil is also believed to treat rheumatoid arthritis, skin sores, and ulcers.

Use in Gris Gris Bags for:
Love, prosperity, protection, repelling negativity

Additional Uses:
It is believed that burning cloves will keep people from gossiping about you.

Interesting Fact:
Cloves are one of many plants used to repel insects.

Crab Apple

The hardy crab apple tree withstands winter's wrath well, making it able to grow throughout the United States (except in the very warm climates of the South and Southwest) and also in Southern Canada. The blossoms that cover the tree later produce fruit resembling tiny apples.

The crab apple was among the Anglo-Saxons' nine sacred herbs in the *Lacnunga*. It was believed to promote deep sleep, increase energy, and speed healing.

Use in Gris Gris Bags for:
Fertility, healing, repelling negativity, sweet dreams

Additional Uses:
Crab apples were used to treat wounds and clear the skin, which may be a reason why they are associated with cleansing spells and repelling negativity.

Interesting Fact:
Crab apples can be used in place of regular apples.

Cypress

The European flame-shaped cypress tree has long been a symbol of death and spiritual immortality. Its durable wood was used in coffins and as mummy cases in Egypt. Its boughs emit a deep fragrance, so the tree may have been chosen for burials to offset the smell of bodily decay.

Cypress is a protective tree as well. It is the perfect tree for ponds and wetlands, helping to stem erosion and purify the soil. In South Louisiana, it is the bald cypress that secures the muddy earth and dispels hurricane storm surges without tipping over.

Plant all types of cypress by your home for protection.

Use in Gris Gris Bags for:
Grief, healing, longevity, protection

Additional Uses:
The lovely scent of cypress was also used as a healing measure.

Interesting Fact:
It is thought that Noah's Ark was constructed from cypress.

Date Palm

The date palm spreads its leaves until a long spindle emerges from the center. Thousands of blossoms appear and slowly ripen into dates; this causes the spindle to lean toward the ground, where hungry visitors can reach the fruit.

Because of its ability to produce an enormous amount of fruit, the date palm has long been associated with fertility and passion. The success of its fruit-bearing also connects it to luck and prosperity spells.

Put the pits of dates inside fertility gris gris bags, or eat a date while creating the bags. Pits can be used in bags for men who wish to restore their sexual potency.

Use in Gris Gris Bags for:
Fertility, luck, passion, prosperity, youth

Additional Uses:
Palm leaves may also be used to promote fertility.

Interesting Fact:
The date palm is one of the five Trees of Life.

Elderberry/Elder

This shrub, which sometimes imitates a tree, is surrounded by numerous myths and superstitions—the consensus being that the wood repels negativity and protects its owner and her home. Elder was a sacred Druid summer solstice tree. It is the symbol of the thirteenth and last month of the *Beth-Luis-Nion* calendar, which ends prior to the winter solstice, and its Celtic Tree Alphabet name is *Ruis*. Just like the old man of the spent year who precedes the baby of each new year, the elder tree is associated with death and rebirth. Elder wood may have been used for Christ's cross (which may be the reason it's never used for cribs).

The elder's leaves, flowers, bark, and berries are all used medicinally. Also called horsetail, elderberry has been used for skin problems and as a digestive aid. The Cajuns and Creoles of South Louisiana believe that a tea made from elderberry flowers will cure a fever. Elder branches have soft centers, and when the centers are removed, the branches make great pop guns for kids. Even though the berries are harmless, the wood is not, as it contains a substance that releases cyanide. Some kids using elder pop guns have become ill, so care must be taken when handling the wood.

Elder is also known as "witchwood," and some believed witches or spirits live within the tree and would be furious with those who used any of the tree without asking permission first. Be sure to ask the tree's permission before using any of its elements.

Use in Gris Gris Bags for:
Death and rebirth, protection, protection against lightning, repelling negativity

Additional Uses:
The tree's bark has been used for a lovely wine that's as delicious as it is good for colds and coughs.

Interesting Fact:
The elder tree doesn't smell particularly good, which is why Shakespeare called it "the stinking elder" in *Cymbeline*. Because of its scent, legends warn not to sleep beneath an elder—it may put you in a coma.

Eucalyptus Tree

There are more than five hundred species of eucalyptus, the majority of them in Australia where the aborigines use them for food and water. The eucalyptus tree's roots are filled with water pulled from the soil, enabling thirsty visitors a reprise on one end of a root if they blow on the other end. Because of this tendency to soak up water, eucalyptus can drain low-lying areas and marshes that breed mosquitoes. Many credited the eucalyptus tree with being a cure for yellow fever (rather than for the absence of mosquitoes) and named it the "fever tree."

Eucalyptus oil is an active germicide, but is used mainly as an expectorant for coughs, asthma, bronchitis, and similar respiratory problems. Many people find relief by breathing the vapors of eucalyptus leaves steeped in boiling water. Burning eucalyptus leaves in a smudge pot or candle ring will produce a similar result.

Use in Gris Gris Bags for:
Healing, protection

Additional Uses:
Eucalyptus is known as an effective insect repellant. We've used its oil on our pets to ward off fleas.

Interesting Fact:
Koalas eat eucalyptus leaves.

Fig Tree

The fig tree is sacred—the symbol of moral teachings and immortality for Buddhists, and a Tree of Life to the Celts. The fig tree plays a role in Genesis, supplying Adam and Eve with clothing (so to speak) after they evoked the wrath of God by eating the forbidden fruit (which some believe was a fig, not an apple). The trees have been cultivated for many thousands of years.

Figs can be used as a sweetener, and they are also highly nutritious. Their expansive, heart-shaped leaves signify love; you may use the leaves to write your desires upon for inclusion in your gris gris bag. You can also grow figs around your home to attract abundance and good fortune.

Use in Gris Gris Bags for:
Divination, fertility, love, prosperity, protection

Additional Uses:
If you dream of a fig tree, prosperity will come and your wishes will be granted.

Interesting Fact:
Fig trees can live up to one hundred years.

Hazel

The hazel tree was sacred to the ancient Celtics, its nuts a representation of wisdom. Legend has it that Fintan, an Irish shaman who could change into any animal, became a salmon and swam under a grove of nine hazel trees. Upon eating the hazelnuts that fell into the water, he acquired great wisdom. Another story claims that Deimne (Fionn), the pupil of the Druid Finegas, caught a salmon and cooked it. When he burned his finger on the salmon's oils, he cooled his finger within his mouth and became wise. And in yet another Celtic legend, Boand approached the well that contained the Salmon of Knowledge, but when she tried to catch one, the well water rose and created a river—the River Boyne, which spread knowledge throughout Ireland.

Eating hazelnuts is thought to open one's mind. And if you dream of a hazelnut, it's a prediction of wealth and unexpected good fortune. The Celtic Tree Alphabet name for the hazel tree is *Coll*.

Use in Gris Gris Bags for:
Creativity, divination, fertility, luck, protection, protection against lightning, wisdom, wishes

Additional Uses:
The Y-shaped twigs of the hazel tree can be used for dowsing.

Interesting Fact:
Hazelnuts are said to provide great inspiration and creativity as well as knowledge (we sampled many, within chocolate, while writing this book).

Holly Tree

Holly is hung around the house at Yule for good luck, its leaves representing the persistence of life in winter. The holly tree is believed to have been used for Christ's crown of thorns and is often called "Christ's Thorns" or "Holy Tree."

Holly leaves are soft in summer, but tough and thorny in winter to keep predators at bay. Since holly defends itself well in winter without losing its color, it has been associated with protection and repelling evil. Pliny the Elder wrote that "holly trees round the house prevent sorcery," and many people believe that if holly grows in your yard after sowing itself, it is a very lucky omen. The Celtic Tree Alphabet name is *Tinne*.

In *As You Like It*, Shakespeare wrote:

> *Heigh-ho! sing, heigh-ho!*
> *unto the green holly*
> *Most friendship is feigning,*
> *most loving mere folly.*
> *Then heigh-ho! the holly!*
> *This life is most jolly.*

Use in Gris Gris Bags for:
Luck, protection, protection against lightning, repelling negativity, sweet dreams

Additional Uses:
Steeped leaves make a good tea for coughs, flus, and fevers.

Interesting Fact:
Holly is used as a symbol of rebirth.

Juniper

Legend has it that if you plant juniper by your front door you will cast away evil spirits, wild animals, and disease, and ward off witches. Native Americans used juniper for its healing qualities, most notably in relieving arthritis, rheumatism, and wounds with poultices and rubs. They incorporated its wood in teepees and fires. Juniper needles make an excellent smudging herb, as well.

The Dutch used this aromatic tree's berries to create gin (the name "juniper" is derived from the Dutch *jenever*). The Druids mixed juniper berries with thyme as an incense.

Use in Gris Gris Bags for:
Healing, protection, repelling negativity

Additional Uses:
Juniper is a diuretic, although not a pleasant-working one.

Interesting Fact:
Juniper berries remove the gamy taste when used as a seasoning for wild game.

Linden
The linden tree's fragrant flowers appear in midsummer and, along with its heart-shaped leaves, are used to treat nervous conditions, colds, headaches, and indigestion. Its wood fiber has been used in making rope, and its blossoms for soothing and softening skin.

Use in Gris Gris Bags for:
Good fortune, love, protection, sweet dreams

Additional Uses:
Hang branches over your door for protection.

Interesting Fact:
Linden produces lovely white and pale yellow flowers with a delicious fragrance, particularly in the south of France.

Mimosa
Many people love the pleasant mimosa tree for its soft leaves, which fold up when touched. But the tree is used for many purposes, including making soaps and perfumes, combating skin and scalp

irritations, fighting wrinkles, and assisting in alleviating nervous tension due to stress.

Many people believe that placing mimosa leaves beneath your pillow will induce sweet dreams.

Use in Gris Gris Bags for:
Healing, love, protection, sweet dreams

Additional Uses:
Boiling dried mimosa leaves and flowers and adding this infusion to a bath is thought to dispel curses and ward off evil.

Interesting Fact:
Mimosa bark is used to tan leather.

Nutmeg Tree

The nutmeg tree produces not a nut, but a seed kernel (inside the fruit) that is dried and grated to use in cooking. We like to use this nutty kernel, however, to string necklaces (with other nuts as well) to ward off rheumatism and other ailments. You can also place a string of nutmeg kernels over a crib to assist with the baby's teething. (Nuts have long been carried as charms and thrown for divination; one way to find out which nuts works best for you is to consider the shape. For instance, a heart-shaped nut may work well in a love gris gris bag.)

Nutmeg also represents fidelity, possibly because it takes nine years for a nutmeg tree to produce its first crop and then it produces kernels consistently for up to seventy-five years. Put nutmeg inside a dream sachet and place it under your pillow to ensure your partner's fidelity (just make sure to use grated nutmeg, not the kernel itself, to avoid lumps!).

Use in Gris Gris Bags for:
Fidelity, healing, love, luck, prosperity

Additional Uses:

Sprinkle ground nutmeg onto a green candle when creating prosperity bags and it will enhance the spell.

Interesting Fact:

Choose your nutmeg kernels and nuts carefully. Sometimes nuts come in unusual shapes, resembling money, hearts, or even the characteristics of your intended.

Oak

The mighty oak, representing strength, endurance and wisdom, was a sacred tree to the Druids, who performed ceremonies beneath its branches. The Greeks also held the oak in esteem, and the Romans dedicated this slow-growing but impressive tree to Jupiter. Its Celtic Tree Alphabet name is *Duir*.

British oak combines toughness with hardness, which makes it an excellent wood for building ships. In America, the live oaks (evergreen oaks) of the coastal South are good for shipbuilding as well, but if you are lucky enough to witness these majestic creatures, their long extended branches dripping with Spanish moss, you'll realize that cutting them down would be a sin. According to the Live Oak Society, an oak by the name of "Seven Sisters" lives outside New Orleans and is estimated to be twelve hundred years old with a thirty-eight-foot girth.

Acorns are a symbol for fertility and can be carried to attract good fortune and acquire strength. Placed in bags and kept in the home, acorns, oak leaves, and oak bark will protect you and invite in the wisdom of your ancestors.

Use in Gris Gris Bags for:

Endurance, fertility, longevity, luck, prosperity, protection, strength, wisdom

Additional Uses:

If you dream of an oak tree, it means wealth and good health are on the way.

Interesting Fact:

It has been said that the Sanskrit word for oak, *deru*, led to the English word "door," which could refer to the perception of the oak as an entry into another world, or into deeper wisdom.

Olive Tree

Like the olive branch, the olive leaf signifies peace. Athenian brides wore olive leaf crowns, which symbolized fertility and love. Olive oil was used for anointing and healing in ancient times, and the extra virgin olive oil available today makes for wonderful, healthy culinary dishes.

Use in Gris Gris Bags for:

Fertility, healing, joy, love, luck, peace

Additional Uses:

Hang olives leaves over your door to encourage peace within the household.

Interesting Fact:

Large olive leaves are said to symbolize good luck.

Orange Tree

Wedding planners often include orange blossoms in garlands and bouquets because of their association with good luck—not to mention their sweet smell, which invokes happiness and love. In gris gris bags, use the peel and seeds of the orange or pick orange blossoms from the tree, particularly when making a love or wedding spell bag.

Orange-flower water has been used in rituals in place of wine, added to love potions and wedding drinks, and placed on altars. Women were said to bathe in orange water to attract the man they wanted to marry, and it was used to flavor foods, notably those prepared for a lover. Orange water is often used in French, North African, and some Middle Eastern cuisines.

Use in Gris Gris Bags for:
Love, luck, good marriage, prosperity

Additional Uses:
Orange peels have oils that help alleviate indigestion, and the grating of the peel produces orange zest, which is used in cooking.

Interesting Fact:
The Chinese view oranges as symbols of good luck and good fortune.

Palmetto

Palmetto palms grow wild in Louisiana. Members of the Houma Indian tribe dry the hearts (hearts of palm), then weave the fronds into beautiful baskets, hats, fans, and mats. In the old days, the Houma used palmetto wood for building their huts. The berries of the saw palmetto can assist men with prostate gland trouble, helping them return to their former sexual prowess. The Seminole Indians in Florida used saw palmetto berries for food (with enhanced sexuality as a side effect) and called these berries the "spring of life."

You can use any variety of palmetto to enhance your gris gris bag.

Use in Gris Gris Bags for:
Passion, protection, repelling negativity

Additional Uses:
Christians in Louisiana use palmetto leaves to make a cross that hangs over the door for protection.

Interesting Fact:
Palmettos especially love bayous and marshes.

Pecan Tree

Early Spanish explorers at Galveston Island, Texas, noted that Native Americans ate pecans, especially during the fall when the nuts are plentiful. The word "pecan," Algonquin in origin, referred to nuts that needed to be cracked open with a rock.

Pecans resemble coins, if you have a good imagination, and can be used in prosperity bags or to gain employment. We always include a small pecan nut in any bag that deals with financial or career issues, but they can be carried in your pocket as well, like a worry stone. Every time you touch the pecan in your pocket, think of what you are working toward and it will come to you.

Use in Gris Gris Bags for:
Employment, prosperity

Additional Uses:
Create a pecan pie and visualize your dream job as you work. No one ever said you can't eat your spells.

Interesting Fact:
The pecan is the state tree of Texas.

Pine

Pine-Sol is a very popular house cleanser, but the practice of cleansing an area with pine has existed for centuries. People would burn pine needles to purify their homes and repel negativity, and pine oil was used as a powerful antiseptic, disinfectant, and air freshener.

Because evergreen pine needles grow in pairs, the pine tree represents permanence in love. Use the needles of any species of pine in love and marriage gris gris bags.

Use in Gris Gris Bags for:
Fertility, good fortune, healing, love, good marriage, prosperity, purification, repelling negativity

Additional Uses:

Pine branches can be hung within houses to attract healing and joy, and in Japan, branches over the doorway ensure continual joy because the needles are evergreen.

Interesting Fact:

There are hundreds of pine varieties.

Rowan

The Celts associated the rowan with protection, and it is considered a magical tree by many. In England, a rowan tree planted by the front door or attached to cattle sheds wards off evil. In Newfoundland, rowan is planted by crops to guard them. Farmers run goats through hooped rowan branches, and rowan twigs are hung over doors to scare off the evil eye. The rowan tree is connected with runes; rune sticks were cut from rowan branches and the symbols carved into the wood. Its Celtic Tree Alphabet name is *Luis.*

The rowan is native to Europe and North American, and also grows as a bush. The white flower of the rowan tree is popular with brides.

Use in Gris Gris Bags for:

Health, love, protection, repelling negativity

Additional Uses:

Rowan berries (red and signifying life) contain vitamins A and C, and the juice can be used as a gargle for sore throats.

Interesting Fact:

The name is linked to the Norse *runa*, meaning charm, and the Sanskrit *runa*, meaning magician.

Walnut Tree

The walnut tree grows large with wide spreading branches, and lives to an old age. Its fruit ripen in mid-September, offering a delicious treat inside a very hard exterior.

These are all good reasons to associate the walnut tree with strength and magic. Many people place a walnut beneath their beds to aid in fertility. The bark of the tree helps heal skin ailments like eczema, and when the nuts are carried, it is thought they ward off heart problems and rheumatism.

Use in Gris Gris Bags for:
Fertility, healing, strength

Additional Uses:
The black walnut tree was used by Native Americans to dispel worms in the body; walnut tinctures make great cleansing agents.

Interesting Fact:
The word "walnut" comes from the Old English word for "foreign nut," because the tree was introduced to England from France and Italy. Its Latin name, *nux Gallica*, translates to "Gaulish nut."

Willow

The willow, a draping tree that resides by water, has been called the Tree of Life in Tibet. It is the Taoist image of strength and flexibility. Because of its association with water, and thus the moon, willows are identified as feminine and used to represent feminine qualities such as childbirth, nurturing, healing, love, and protection. Its Celtic Tree Alphabet name is *Saille* (meaning "bright").

The Druids used willow branches for wands and staffs.

Use in Gris Gris Bags for:
Fertility, healing, love, protection, strength

Additional Uses:
Willow bark has been used to relieve fevers, headaches, and rheumatism, and is what led to our modern aspirin.

Interesting Fact:
Sitting under willows is supposed to inspire inspiration and prophecies.

Witch Hazel

The witch hazel tree, native to the eastern United States, is best known for setting its own schedule and blooming in late fall or winter. This shrublike tree is also known as "snapping hazelnut" because its seedpods open with a popping sound, and the seeds are projected ten to twenty feet.

The "witch" in the name likely derives from the Middle English *wyche*, meaning "flexible" or "pliant." Although the tree is not related to hazel, early American settlers used its branches as divining rods to find water underground ("water witching"), just as hazel twigs were used in England.

Use in Gris Gris Bags for:
Healing, peace, protection

Additional Uses:
When used in a poultice, witch hazel reduces bruising and swelling, sprains, insect bites, and bleeding.

Interesting Fact:
Witch hazel is often used in deodorants.

Yew

The yew, sacred to the ancient Druids, reaches its roots deep into the ground to create new stems and new life, even when the trunk of the tree decays and dies. In essence, a new tree grows within the old. This reincarnation has led to legends about the yew as the middle ground between life on Earth and the otherworld. For centuries, the yew has been planted in churchyards for this very reason, always as a symbol of death and rebirth, new life springing from the old. Its Celtic Tree Alphabet name is *Iodhadh*.

Indigenous to England, yews are one of the oldest trees on earth. The Crowhurst Yew in Surrey, England, is estimated to be between one thousand and four thousand years old.

Use in Gris Gris Bags for:
Death and rebirth, longevity, strength

Additional Uses:
As a symbol of rebirth, yew is a great ingredient for spells that aim to get rid of bad habits or beliefs and start anew.

Interesting Fact:
Yews are highly poisonous, but the shoots and berries are sometimes used in homeopathy.

STONES & CRYSTALS
· · · · · · · · · · · · · · · ·

Our Earth is a work in progress. Her face changes with every wind, and her core is a percolating heart that is constantly feeding itself. The magic that rises from the Earth takes a multitude of forms, the most common being that of stones and crystals. Whether manifesting in the massive outcroppings of sandstone that undulate for miles, or in the tiniest pebble sleeping on the ocean floor, each stone is a revelation of the Earth's excellence and ingenuity. Within the heart of each stone beats the heart of the Earth.

Plentiful, colorful, and variable, stones and crystals come in more shapes and sizes than we can ever imagine. They are perfect combinations of intention and resolve, their creation blended with wind, air, and water. Honed to a state of molecular excellence, they flaunt their blemishes, imperfect representations of perfection. Each stone's colors disclose its purpose and can guide you in how to use it: as clear quartz, a stone can dazzle; as a garnet, it flushes a fiery red; as a sky-blue turquoise, it soothes; as pyrite, it sparkles with the golden intention of riches. There are meanings upon meanings in every stone. Their shapes speak of origins, and each stone beneath our feet—whether balanced on a mountain ledge or dancing on a swirling shoreline—holds immeasurable magic.

Various stones, shells, and sea glass can be included in your gris gris bag.

Over millions of years, stones have continued their quest. They warm as they pull in heat from the sun, and cool as they draw the chill from the Earth's surface. They erupt in monolithic majesty and hold imprints in their memories, testaments to history. They carry the mysteries of the universe, and tell the tales of the Earth in painstaking detail. Even as they are reduced to the tiniest fragment of themselves, they bond with others and become a handful of sand, a milky white beach, or the fine silt of the ocean floor. They are the foundation of the Earth—bedrock holding the surface together, and sedimentary stones entering into cohesive marriages to form newer stones of many properties. Stones never really go away; if nothing else, they are symbols of physical eternity.

So it stands to reason that stones and crystals are vital elements to include in your gris gris bag. Whatever your intention, there is a stone for your need. Just remember that stones are truly our ancestors. Regardless of their origin, how you locate them, or their physical beauty, the stones you work with will contain wonders.

Woti

The Lakota Native American tribe believes in what is known as a *Woti* (pronounced "woe-tie") stone. This tradition holds that a stone can connect uniquely to an individual, and that the stone and the person's soul find each other. The stone doesn't have to be polished or full of vibrancy, and it certainly isn't expensive (since it's "found"). It's as if both you and the stone have been on a journey to connect, and when you find each other, you know it. These are the best stones to include in your gris gris bags—the simple, found stones that seem to sing more loudly than all those around them.

When you connect with a stone, spend time with it. Hold it in one hand, then the other. Let the energy of the stone completely connect with your energy, and let it tell you why it has come into your life. This might take a certain amount of concentration, especially if you've never worked with stones before.

One thing to think about is where you found the stone. Did it come from the beach? Was it washed up during a violent storm, or gently deposited on the shoreline by methodical, lapping waves, arriving at its destination with assurance and purpose? Imagine the history of your stone. Has it sprung from the deepest depths of the Earth's core, or found its way here from some magnificent celestial occurrence ten million years ago? It's hard to imagine the lifetime of a stone.

Purchased Stones

Stones that come with a designated purpose, like those purchased in a metaphysical store or through a gem or rock dealership, are equally magnificent. These are the polished varieties mentioned so prominently in dozens of metaphysical guides. There are the simple stones such as rose quartz, whose pink color is strongly indicative of lasting love, and hematite, whose unique metal-like appearance speaks of protection and healing, and also stones with far more complex magical elements, such as celestite and moldavite. Celestite, a sparkling, pale blue crystal, is magnificently hypnotic. Its soothing color induces a sense of peace and focus in those looking at it. It's one of the many stones that are useful in chakra cleansing. Moldavite, an intensely dark and mysterious celestial stone, is also effective for chakra cleansing and good for expediting spiritual evolution and protection. Both of these stones can work well within your spell pouch, depending on your intention.

There are many reference books to guide you to the nuanced properties of the hundreds of stones available. One thing to keep in mind, however, is to avoid putting a stone that has too many profound properties into a bag that has a simple intention. This can serve to diffuse the focus of the bag, rather than enhance it.

Selecting Your Crystals and Stones

The key to selecting the right stones or crystals for a specific gris gris bag is, first of all, color. While plants tend to communicate their magical properties through physical interactions with us, a stone's magical properties are quite subtle; color is one of the few indicators to its properties. For example, consider the energy of a green stone. Green surrounds us in the natural world. Every shade imaginable appears in trees, shrubs, and even the ocean—and every shade imaginable appears in stones. Rich emerald green, deep forest green, and lively kelly green all speak to us in one way or another, and they all have a distinctive story to tell. Of course, as well as this connection with nature, green stones have also become associated with wealth. Meanwhile, blue stones often indicate peace, serenity, and meditation, as is so clearly illustrated by the blue sky. Look up, either during the peak of day or in the depths of night, and sense the connection we have to the blues that surround us all the time.

Another thing to keep in mind is that each stone has a specific organic makeup that defines its purpose. Whether the crystals that form the stone are granule, hexagonal, in fibrous layers, spiked, or erratic determines the essence of the stone. Remember that all stones are products of that greater being: the universe. Some come from the sky, while others are honed by the magic of the ocean or fashioned by the persistent wind.

Overall, though, the best way to select a stone for your intention is to consider what the color and shape of the stone mean to you *personally*. Creating your gris gris bag is a personal experience. You will begin infusing intention into the bag from the moment you select the pouch itself, and this intention continues as you compile each and every ingredient. If the bag is being created as a gift, then its intention becomes even greater, enhanced by the power of giving and love. The stones you select contain the innate energy of the Earth; whether you found them, purchased them, or received them as a gift, they hold within them the magic of tens of thousands of years of existence. Honor them for the wisdom they impart, and remember that they are intimately connected to your intention as the bag's creator. It is a beautiful, symbiotic relationship.

The list below describes some of the key types of stones to incorporate in your gris gris bags. These suggestions are based on our personal experiences. Most of the stones listed are plentiful and inexpensive. Many come in several colors, with their purpose differentiated accordingly. As mentioned above, you can purchase your stones in metaphysical shops, but found stones (like other found elements) are the best ones to include.

Agate

Since agates are common and available in a variety of colors, it is important to remember your intention and how it connects to color when selecting an agate. The stone is actually made of various types of chalcedony, a quartz mineral. It is named for the Sicilian river Achetes (now named Drillo), where it is commonly found. We find the fire agate the most attractive because of its rich red tones that signify creativity and sexuality, both powerful forces. Other colors available in agate include blue lace, holly blue, dendritic (which is not banded like most agates), crazy lace, black banded, Chinese golden, moss, white, yellow, and purple sage.

Amber

Calling amber a "stone" is a misnomer—it is actually made up of ancient fossilized resins, and often contains residue from prehistoric times, including insect and plant parts. Therefore, a piece of amber contains the elemental energy of those plants and insects, locked in time for millions of years. Be sure to keep this history in mind as you formulate your intention.

The ancient Greeks called amber *elektron*, meaning "sun," and its properties have been likened to the sun. Significantly warm, amber exudes an intense healing energy and it is said to aid in battling depression and other psychological disorders. Since it contains the pure and persistent energies of plant life, it serves well for purification, much like trees purify our air. Also, its vivid organic history helps us connect to our own ancestral paths.

Amethyst

This is the perfect comfort stone, which many people turn to when feeling exceptionally vulnerable. Plentiful and inexpensive, amethyst is popular because of its rich, purple, crystalline appearance. Simply looking at an amethyst has a distinctively soothing effect. We all have periods of our lives when we feel overwhelmed or out of control. Amethyst is also the perfect stone to help with divine connection and aid you in releasing physical addictions. It is also known for its cleansing properties.

Aquamarine

Aptly named for its ocean-blue color, the aquamarine is a gorgeous, highly prized stone that has soothing, cooling properties. It is said to aid in communication, and therefore would be an effective addition to your gris gris bag if your intention involves opening lines of communication and eliminating misinterpretation. Aquamarine also helps free up the creative process and the ability to convey ideas and concepts more clearly. The connection aquamarine has with the ocean helps personal empowerment by connecting the user to universal life energies. It has natural cleansing properties as well.

Aventurine

We most often use aventurine as a money-draw stone. Although it is available in blue and red, it is most commonly found in a soft green. It also can bring optimism and confidence to the bearer and help you keep pace when life becomes challenging. This stone's enhancement properties combine well with other stones, and it contains natural healing energies because of its ability to promote renewal. Blue aventurine contains the same core properties as green, although it speaks more to the spiritual level and aids in psychic alignment. The red variety connects with our creative and sexual lives.

Azurite

Azurite is one of our personal favorites. Its rich cobalt blue color speaks of mystery, and its general properties include insight, intuition, and intellect. It is excellent for clearing or cleansing the third-eye chakra. You may use this stone for meditation at night before going to sleep, or add as an ingredient in a dream pillow. It enhances one's sense of spiritual expansion as you relax your body from this plane of existence into the realm of sleep. You'll find that it helps release the tensions of the day and helps you focus entirely on peace. It is said to be effective for ailments involving the head, including migraines.

Bloodstone

The bloodstone is a simple chalcedony that is distinguished by a green color embellished with threads or flecks of red. The red is rich and bloodlike, hence the name. Also as indicated in its name, bloodstone signifies vitality, strength, and bravery. If your intention for a gris gris bag is to connect the user to any of these types of characteristics, then bloodstone is an excellent choice. If the user is facing difficult circumstances and seeking strength, whether spiritual, physical, emotional, or intellectual, this stone will bind to that intention and assist them with their goals. It is also a good stone for diffusing negative influences.

Carnelian

This enticing red/orange stone speaks to sexuality. Linked to vitality and creativity, it can help awaken sleeping ambition and bring the user to a place of action, action, and more action. If you're exploring a new direction, career, or relationship, this is the ideal stone to which you should bind your intentions.

Celestite

Another favorite of ours, this stone's beautiful sky-blue color can help connect you to a higher dimension and promote angelic communication.

Celestite has a unique clarity that is invariably enticing to anyone seeking its powers. It tends to come in larger pieces with breathtakingly beautiful crystalline formations, so it doesn't always lend itself to the inclusion within a bag, but it can serve as a facilitator to your intentions when you are assembling the bag. This is an excellent stone for connecting with your spiritual or angelic guides and asking for their assistance.

Citrine

This beautiful stone gets its yellow tint from a high iron content, and its name is derived from the French word for lemon, *citron*. It is sometimes used as a money draw, in accordance with the belief that placing stones in the inside corners of your home will attract fortune. Small pieces may be included in a gris gris bag to help manifest your desires.

Citrine was popular in ancient times for aiding mental clarity and creativity, and it's an ideal stone for sharpening intellectual skills and enhancing the thinking process. Include this stone in a bag if your intention is to help with problem solving.

Emerald

Emeralds are said to connect to the heart chakra and stimulate love and compassion as well as abundance, which is clearly expressed by their rich green color. A traditional gift stone, emerald's ability to stimulate love also promotes healing in that area. If you're creating a bag for someone nursing a broken heart or any type of emotional loss, placing an emerald in their gris gris bag will greatly enhance that intention.

Like many precious stones, emeralds are graded by color (shades of green), tone (translucency), and clarity (inclusions/impurities). For the purpose of the gris gris bag, using a low-grade, raw emerald is fine. These are available through metaphysical stores and online, for about the same price as quartz crystal and amethyst; the higher-grade emeralds are cost prohibitive and usually only available through a jeweler.

Flint

Composed of silica, this plentiful stone truly comes from the heart of the Earth. Ancient peoples used flint to craft arrowheads and other tools. The fact that its surface fractures conchoidally (smooth ridges and depressions) made it a perfect choice for creating cutting instruments, since it can be easily honed into sharp, knifelike edges.

Flint is known for aiding in self-discipline and for forging connections between the physical and spiritual planes. Along these lines, it helps with visualizing the clear connections between the two worlds and better utilizing aspects of spirituality within our physical lives. Overall, this very matter-of-fact stone stimulates our practical nature while also allowing us to embrace our ethereal truth.

Garnet

This stone is usually a rich, vibrant red, though it does appear in other colors, including green, amber, and black. Because of its rich color and depth, garnet is also one of our favorite stones. Its appearance alone stimulates creative thought, and it can aid in visualization practices. The red signifies its connection with passionate love. Prosperity is also a key property of garnet, and it has within it the power to help you make whatever you imagine become reality. It therefore makes a nice addition if you're building a bag for someone who is looking to fire up their creative side.

Hematite

We use this stone primarily for protection, though it has many other properties. Its unique energies serve to diffuse negative vibrations that may attach to us throughout the day, and it can be an excellent choice for overall healing. Sometimes magnetized, hematite usually is metallic black or gray and is said to aid in grounding in the physical plane. It can help guide you toward a feeling of unity, bringing together what would normally be considered opposing energies. If you're struggling with ambivalence, hematite can help you make a decision.

Jade

Jade's properties are as diverse as its colors, a result of the stone being composed of two different types of minerals. Green jade is the most common, and is associated with health, wealth, and abundance. The rich green hues, echoing those found in nature, strongly indicate its wonderful healing properties. Purple jade is a more spiritual stone than its green counterpart, while black jade offers protection and red jade inspires action and bravery. Blue jade brings us back to the spiritual realm, and also enhances clarity of thought.

Jasper

One of the many multi-colored stones available, jasper has a variety of properties. Picture jasper gets its name from how its bands and swirls of color seem to create a picture of a desert landscape; mook jasper has swirls of yellow and/or white in a red base. Unakite jasper, marbleized with a palette of pinks, greens, and grays, stimulates a number of energies, including balance, healing, and the cleansing of both physical and spiritual toxins. Even single-colored jasper (red, brown, green, or yellow) has distinctive angular markings that harken back to the name, a French/Latin derivative meaning "speckled stone."

In many ways, jasper seems to be a message from the Earth itself. Because of this unique connection with the Earth, it contains similar properties: tenacity, strength, stability, and self-healing. It can also aid with grounding.

Jet

A type of coal, jet is easily recognized by its opaque black appearance and light weight. It is a wonderful protection and purifying stone, and has been called "the witch's stone" because of its mysterious and powerful properties. Many pagan practitioners rely on jet to help quell negative energies and transform them into positive energies.

Because jet (a mineraloid derived from decayed wood) is made primarily of carbon—the chemical base of all life, and the second-most abundant element in the human body—it speaks directly to our core. It tends to enhance overall energy regardless of your specific intention for the stone; in this sense, jet is a good universal stone.

Labradorite

Originally named for its location of origin (the Labrador Peninsula in Canada), this stone comes in a wide variety of colors and can be quite breathtaking. It's known as a markedly magical stone, in that it can help users access their deepest magical abilities and aid them in magical focus. Labradorite makes a wonderful addition to a gris gris bag designed for the enhancement of powers, but it can also help the bag-maker amplify their intention as they construct the bag.

Lapis Lazuli

Often used in jewelry and favored by the ancient Egyptians, lapis lazuli is a regal powder-blue color. It is said to connect the user to their psychic abilities and stimulate one's intuitive nature. Because it was placed in so many tombs to adorn bodies and usher souls to the next world, some believe that lapis lazuli connects us to the spirit world, allowing communication with those who have crossed over. It's therefore a perfect stone to use in bags where the advice of spirit guides, ancestors, or angels would come in handy.

Lodestone

Comprised of naturally magnetic iron ore, the lodestone has long been heralded as highly magical because of its powerful magnetic nature. Lodestones are identified as male or female based on their shape, so when paired (that is, a male and female stone carried together), lodestones can attract enduring love. (Same-sex stones can also attract, based on their magnetic qualities.) Those lodestones that cannot be matched due to an odd shape can be used as all-around good luck charms, effective in drawing money and good fortune.

Lodestones are readily available and inexpensive. Their effectiveness can be enhanced when combined with magnetic sand. Since lodestone is useful for increasing your power of attraction, try to keep your thoughts positive when carrying one or using one in a gris gris bag.

Malachite

A beautiful green stone with oceanic striations waving through it, the malachite's strongest attributes are those of protection and creativity. It protects the bearer from taking on negative or complex energies from outside sources, and it clears the way for a more direct path toward satisfaction of the creative self. It can help create balance within your core, and heal the heart. It can stimulate motivation and is an excellent stone to use for overcoming procrastination. Despite its green color, drawing wealth is only a small aspect of this beautiful stone's power.

Meteorite

There are various types of meteorites, with various components, but they are most commonly composed of iron. Regardless of their composition, however, the fact that these stones traveled through the galaxy gives them exceptional powers. The fact that they made it to the Earth's surface is a miracle in itself, and this tenacity bespeaks a meteorite's innate qualities. As with any other stone, imagine its history as you bind your intention to it.

Meteorite is excellent for connecting with the spiritual and celestial (or heavenly) plane and promoting expansive thinking. It can help you overcome fear of traveling, encouraging self-sufficiency and the sense of adventure. It brings with it the wisdom of the universe.

Moldavite

This deep green, glassy stone has mysterious origins. It is believed to be a common stone that was altered by the crash of a meteorite. Regardless, moldavite speaks clearly to the user. Its enormous power can help elevate you to the spiritual realm, and it encourages a greater understanding of all things mysterious. It is believed to have been a favored amulet among prehistoric peoples in Eastern Europe, where it was first found and named.

Moldavite affects each of us in different ways and can vary vastly— this is the nature of an innately powerful stone. Legend speaks of it having the power to physically alter reality. Moldavite is not a stone to be taken lightly; we recommend that you work with it for a few days in order to connect with its inherent nature, so that you can make the best use of it while building your bag. Moldavite can be pricey, but it is well worth the investment.

Moonstone

The moonstone is full of mystery, much like the moon itself. It can offer the bearer deeper insight into their personal spiritual realm. Using a moonstone during meditation can enrich and expedite the process, bringing you to a greater depth of awareness. It aids in the path to self-awareness as well, and will "shine light" on your true nature, the good with the bad. If patience is an issue for you, a moon-stone can help quell anxiousness and bring about a greater under-standing of the concept *all things in due time.*

Directly connected to the moon's feminine energies, moonstone stimulates the maternal nature in all of us, male or female. It is also known as the "traveler's stone" and is carried on journeys for pro-tection and good fortune. It comes in a variety of colors, including white, gray, and peach, and its opalescence makes it appealing for use in jewelry. To recharge this stone, place it under the light of a full moon.

Obsidian

Obsidian is a perfect protection stone, well-known for dispelling negative energies. It is available in several colors—snowflake (white flecks), mahogany (rich red striations), and rainbow or peacock (where strong light reveals hidden colors)—but its core is a rich, dark mystery. It can be used for grounding and spiritual communication, and thus covers a wide range of energies, but its protection and healing powers reign paramount.

Onyx

A stalwart stone, indicative of inner strength, onyx has a rich density that signifies its nature. Its colors vary (although black is the most common), and it can appear markedly different when its bands are revealed, but onyx projects a sense of control, infusing the user with added power and resolve as they face life's challenges. It brings about a sense of calm and can quell anxiousness, helping you to maintain focus. A plentiful and inexpensive stone, onyx is a good addition to a gris gris bag for someone who is feeling frustrated about a lack of control or direction in their lives.

Opal

The fire opal erupts with a beautiful brilliance that articulates passion and creativity; the white opal has a mystical rainbow appearance, indicating the powerful spiritual energy it contains. This stone is most commonly known for its use in jewelry. If you chose to put one in your bag, seek out an opal that speaks to your personal energy. Opals are so varied and have such diverse levels of vibration that it's best to clearly consider your intention and let the stone connect directly to you. As a highly emotionally charged stone, opals will stimulate the emotions of the user—when used properly, they can bring about inner peace, and help keep things in perspective for someone facing a challenging period in their lives.

Peridot

These sparkling, pale green gems are highly positive and can shine an encouraging light on even the most dire circumstances. Peridot's innate energy acts as a driving force, infusing us with the fearlessness to face difficult tasks. It is also useful in guiding us to a better understanding of ourselves and our inherent flaws, and in learning how to forgive ourselves for past mistakes. Also, just looking at a peridot will make you think of wealth and gain; it is an excellent prosperity stone.

Petrified Wood

This is another one of our all-time favorites because it represents two elements—stone and wood—that have magically become one. Since every tree contains a spirit, the spirit of the fossilized tree still exists within the petrified wood. Although it is impossible to identify the specific kind of tree that a piece of petrified wood came from, the essence of the tree remains. Therefore, petrified wood carries a two-fold magic: magic from both stone and tree.

Petrified wood is effective for recalling past lives, and helps if you have baggage left over from a previous existence. It can also help dispel irrational fears. This stone speaks of eternal life—even when total transformation is necessary, the soul remains.

Pyrite

Because of its gold-like appearance, this stone is most commonly known as "fool's gold." This, however, is a misnomer. Though not as rare as actual gold, pyrite's properties are of great value. Plentiful and magnificent, this stone can incite action and confidence; it will stimulate the user to move forward from a state of stagnation.

Quartz Crystal (clear)

This is a universal energy stone. It helps the user focus their intention and draw in the energy necessary to make things come to fruition. It is a versatile and personal stone. When selecting a quartz crystal to work with, hold it in your hand and feel the vibrations. Since every crystal is different, your unique connection to it is vital.

Small quartz points are an excellent addition to any gris gris bag. They draw energy into the bag and promote a symbiotic relationship between the various ingredients.

Rose Quartz

As the pink (or rose) version of quartz, rose quartz is a warm and friendly stone anxious to help you on your quest for love. It can help reduce the stress attached to desire and allow for a free flow of energy that will help bring about your intention. This stone is plentiful and inexpensive. We keep large pieces of it throughout the house to promote a loving and stress-free atmosphere. It can clear away emotional baggage while helping heal the heart, preparing it to move to a new level of emotional awareness. Rose quartz should be included in any gris gris bag dealing with enduring love.

Ruby

The vibrant red of a ruby immediately brings to mind passion, coupled with the courage to move forward with any challenge. Although rubies are never green, their immense drawing power can bring prosperity of all kinds to the user. Their powerful energy encourages a feeling of universal contentment as well, helping you connect with the true joy of living on this Earthly plane while also remaining connected to the spiritual plane. Rubies also stimulate bravery and the desire to protect those weaker than ourselves.

This stone is a magnificent addition to a bag prepared for someone who has let fear create stagnancy in their lives. As with other precious stones, there are varying grades of rubies, which affects cost (see the discussion in the emerald entry).

Salt

Once prized for its scarcity, salt is now one of the most common minerals on Earth, thanks to advanced mining and extraction methods. Frequently used during religious rituals, salt contains a number of healing properties and is excellent for purification. Because of the varying chemical compositions of different salts, it can have different nuances to its intention. But as a key element of ocean water, one of salt's essential qualities is its connection to the existence of life on Earth. Overall, salt is a good addition to a gris gris bag to clear away the erratic energies of other items in the bag and balance the effect.

Selenite

Milky white, selenite has a natural column-like shape that gives it the feel of a wand. But this stone acts more like an antenna, since one of its important properties is its ability to facilitate angelic communication. Like salt, it is an effective cleansing stone, blazing an energy path through the complex vibrations of the Earth and straight into the ethereal plane. A very soft mineral, it can be found in colors other than white, but its properties remain the same.

This stone can draw in such powerful energies that many users claim to feel physical changes almost immediately. Small shards of selenite in your gris gris bag can help quickly connect your intention to higher energies.

Serpentine

Serpentine comes in a variety of colors, often green, and its name alludes to the similarity of the stone's surface to the mottled skin of a serpent. It is an unusual stone because it is so exclusively connected to the Earth. Unlike the many stones known for bridging the gap between the physical world and the ethereal one, serpentine is content to sing the praises of the Earth in all her glory. If our planet had veins like our bodies do, the veins would be made of serpentine.

While serpentine can be used to clear an energy path, it is primarily a physical stone and invites the user to explore their personal spiritual connection to the Earth. Also, serpentine in your gris gris bag can awaken the innate energies of the other items and encourage cohesiveness as the bag works toward the intended goal.

Smoky Quartz

An excellent stone for grounding, smoky quartz dispels negative energy and reminds us, as we're on our spiritual journey, that physical existence must also be tended as part of the quest. It can help the great procrastinator get on with things, and help the distracted user become more organized and efficient, fearlessly gaining control over the controllable things in their life.

Aligning your focus in the physical plane can be instrumental in manifesting your true desires. In a gris gris bag, smoky quartz serves as a reminder to address what is necessary before moving on to the next phase of your adventure.

Staurolite

Staurolite tends to be a bit expensive because of its unusual formation—it contains prismatic crystals that, where they meet, form the shape of a cross. This image, long lauded as a spiritual icon in various faiths, erupts from a pale gray base. The cross can be distinct, but is more often distorted; the degree to which it is distinct determines the price of the stone.

Staurolite is an amazing stone to work with while assembling a bag, although not necessarily a practical addition to the pouch itself. It's a good grounding stone, and can be used to eliminate bad habits and dispel irrational fears. Some believe staurolite aids in connecting with alternative dimensions or spiritual realms.

Tiger's Eye

The mysterious brown and gold swirls of this stone fit perfectly with its name. Tiger's eye speaks of the strength and stamina of the tiger, prompting the user to resist hesitation and act when ready, facing challenges fearlessly. Tiger's eye is also an excellent balancing stone, and effective for insight and guidance. It is as enigmatic as an eye … when you bind your mutual powers, it feels as though there is a life coursing through the stone. It infuses your gris gris with the energy to distinguish what is necessary from what can be ignored.

Tourmaline

Since tourmaline comes in a variety of colors, the best way to select your stone is based on the color. From black for protection to red for love, tourmaline can support things as diverse as higher consciousness, healing, communication, and inner strength. Align your intention, your bag color, your candle color, and the other elements when building your gris gris, then chose the tourmaline that feels right for you. This remarkably powerful stone makes a strong addition to any bag.

Turquoise

A familiar stone because of its wide usage in Native American cultures, turquoise is noted for its aqua blue hue. It makes wonderful jewelry. Found in ancient civilizations across the globe, this stone is said to aid the user in spiritually empowering themselves. It helps us recognize our purpose while we temporarily dwell on the physical plane. So use turquoise in your gris gris if you are aiding someone who has lost direction or is seeking guidance from a higher level.

Vanadinite

This rare, unusual red stone is linked to the root chakra and associated with sexual and creative energy. Often we don't recognize the connection between sexuality and creativity, but sexuality is the precursor to giving birth, the ultimate creative act we have as human beings. Vanadinite is effective in enhancing creativity, and can award the user with clarity and vitality. This can be a powerful aid for getting things done, if your intention is to see results.

Vanadinite tends to be both pricey and fragile. It is therefore not always a practical addition to a gris gris bag, but if you have small fragments that have broken off a piece of vanadinite, adding them to the bag will seriously enhance the intention of creative motivation. Vanadinite also makes an ideal gift for someone who is blocked creatively, to help clear away the cobwebs and stimulate their innate creative soul.

METALS, SHELLS & BONES
· · · · · · · · · · · · · · · ·

Other items for your gris gris bag can range from metals to shells to bones. As with stones, it is best to allow the object to speak to you. If you are drawn to something as simple as a coin, then include it. Often coins bring wealth, regardless of denomination, because they are infused with that intention from their inception and have been used in barter and exchange over time. With metals especially, there are a variety of properties to consider when adding them to a gris gris bag.

Gold

Because of its color, gold is representative of all the properties of the sun. It is spiritually linked to solar energy and conveys power, confidence, and control. The sun is the center and overseer of our solar system and is essential to life as we know it; it is linked to energies of the greater good and is cleansing, revitalizing, and energizing. Using gold flecks in your gris gris can help connect the bearer with their own greater purpose.

Copper

Our personal favorite metal, copper is best known for its conductive properties. Although gold contains the strongest conductive energy, copper combines the color of earth (a rich brown) with the essence of the sun, thus bringing completion to any intention by connecting the ethereal world with the physical one. Copper is also effective for healing. Energy passes through it with ease, so copper also serves to enhance the intention within a bag.

Magnetic Sand

This is a very powerful enhancement tool when added to any spell or gris gris bag. Its magnetic properties draw your desires to you; it should not be used when your intention is to rid yourself of something. Magnetic sand is actually the iron ore content in ocean sand

and can be easily harvested from the sea. Like sea glass, it is infused with the powers and energies inherent to the ocean. Magnetic sand can be used in conjunction with lodestones to enhance their power of attraction.

Silver

Silver embodies the moon's shining face in the night sky. It is an emotional metal and can be used to quell erratic feelings. Effective during menopause, silver soothes fiery tension. It is an excellent abundance metal, but those properties are secondary to its underlying ability to bring balance to severely unbalanced situations.

Shells

Like most naturally occurring objects, shells are made from once-living material. They consist primarily of calcium, much like human bones, and are the exoskeleton of the mollusk they once housed. The origins of shells points to their connection to the organic world and their similarity with human existence.

Shells may be selected by their color, though many are often bleached white by the sea and sun. There are different types of shells, some very common while others are prized more for their rarity than for their metaphysical properties.

The *clamshell* speaks of abundance and speed, while a *mussel* is usually black and purple and is more indicative of tenacity and strength. Plentiful shells, like *barnacles*, are suspension feeders and will attach themselves to their substrates for the duration of their lives. (These shells are useful when trying to rid oneself of a stubborn or clingy person, but be sure to make use of them during a waning moon.) *Scallop shells* can be brightly colored and very desirable, but are not as easy to find in one piece. They can bring beauty to one's life, if that is the intention, and their fan shape indicates their ability to evade capture. Scallop shells are also useful when your intention is to avoid unpleasantness or to assure success in legal or professional matters. Some of the more decorative shells, such as *conch*, *spindle*, and *trumpet shells*, may be selected based on their unique shapes. For example, a trumpet shell can be used to enhance communication with another person, or to help you be heard. Conch shells, because of their wrapped appearance, aid in protecting secrets, but also may indicate warmth and security, as in a house blessing.

The *cowrie shell* once belonged to the sea snail, and most commonly sports a yellow crown and is used for luck and protection. Cowrie shells with a purple crown have the same attributes but stronger power. They are used in divination—with thirteen shells, you can ask simple yes/no questions. When the shells turn their smooth backs up, it indicates "yes," but if their opening faces up, it indicates "no." In many cultures, the cowrie shell is a symbol of fertility; the egg shape is indicative of a pregnant woman, while the underside resembles the vulva. This makes the cowrie shell an excellent choice for a gris gris made for someone wishing to conceive a child. Over the centuries and by many cultures, cowrie shells were often used as currency. Because of their porcelain appearance and desirable color, they are prized as jewelry. Thus, the cowrie may also be used for wealth, abundance, and overall enrichment. Use cowrie shells in your gris gris bags for luck, protection, fertility, prosperity, enrichment of the soul, and material gain.

Please remember, as you search for shells, that it is not at all necessary to use only whole, unbroken shells in your gris gris bags. And please do not feel the need to sacrifice a sea creature in order to garner a shell. There are plenty of empty or broken shells available. If you collect small pieces of shells, however, it may be difficult to discern which creature the shell originated from. In such a case, appreciate the pieces for what the ocean has infused them with and allow the ocean's energy to be your primary focus.

Another ocean gift is the *sand dollar*. These creatures dwell just beneath the surface and when the animal dies, it leaves behind its skeleton, known as a "test," which becomes dried by the sun. This dried "shell" can bring good luck, protection, and prosperity. Its round appearance earned the sand dollar its name, but it is the animals' essence that hints of magical properties. When living, they often dwell in clusters in soft, sandy regions. They have a pentamerous symmetry; in other words, they consist of five parts, and have markings that are unique. The mythos of the number five adds to their magic—five is the number of vision and adventure. So, if you're building a bag for someone yearning for freedom and the courage to move in a new direction, a piece of a sand dollar could add a needed stimulus to their bag.

Coral, in all its many colors and incarnations, is associated with the moon and the feminine spirit. Working with coral is very similar to working with bones—when alive, coral is a complex, thriving entity vital to the delicate balance of the ocean's ecostructure. It is capable of communicating within its own species and reproduces both asexually and via spawning. (Do not harvest living coral yourself under any circumstances—it is a protected species.) Dead, or bleached, coral structures are available through the Internet and at beachfront shops, and occasionally can be found along the shoreline. If you choose to use coral in your gris gris, be sure to thank the universe for this gift and recognize the amazing energy you are placing within the bag. Many cultures employed coral as a protective amulet, and Italian women used it to help regulate menstrual flow (especially red coral, which was believed to contain divine blood or the essence of life). Coral can also be used to promote healing and a sense of peace, and to bring the wearer joy and happiness. It is commonly utilized to safeguard children, as a traveler's amulet (especially if traveling by sea), and to promote sweet dreams if placed beneath a pillow.

Sea glass, although not a shell, can bring a much needed boost to your gris gris bags. These random pieces of found glass are honed by the ocean and infused with her spirit. They can be almost any color and often have a frosted look from the oceans' salty, fiercely gentle massage. When considering a piece of sea glass, color is paramount in your selection.

Bones

Bones bespeak the dead. They carry echoes of the spirit that once animated them. As the frame that cradles the soul, they are the final remains when all other pretenses have been shed. The fact that human bones continue to produce stem cells throughout their entire lifetime, not just during early development, is living proof that we are continually renewed—as our spirits grow and change during life, so does the vessel. Bones are the quintessence of magic.

It stands to reason that nearly all ancient cultures viewed bones as sacred. While the spirit may be eternal, that which is left behind on Earth must carry some lingering essence. Bones still hold the nature of the animal, embracing the inherent strengths of each beast. They are complex in design and strong in quality. For thousands of years, native cultures throughout the globe adorned themselves with bones, often stringing them as necklaces or using them in piercings. Bones can be honed as tools, sewn into traditional dress, or used to embellish an altar. They have been used for divination, protection, and as assurances of health or long life.

The bones gathered for a gris gris bag should have special meanings that help manifest the intention of the bearer. The lingering essence of the bones will bind with the other ingredients in the bag to bring about change. But given their powerful qualities, select your bones cautiously. Definitely do not ever kill a creature just to use its bones in your gris gris. Bones from naturally fallen animals are best, and ideally, from animals who met a peaceful end. Energy is present in the psychic memory of the bones, so a traumatic experience may linger and give bones a negative essence.

Also be sure to consider the type of bone in light of your intention. If you are creating a bag for protection while traveling, you might select a femur, the large thigh bone. If strength and resolve are your focus, consider the vertebra. Consider as well the type of animal your bone comes from; antler pieces may serve well in a sachet designed for protection and renewal.

TALISMANS

· · · · · · · · · · · · · · ·

A talisman is simply a decorative magical object. What we like so much about the idea of talismans is that they are unique to their purpose. They come purely from personal inspiration as you connect to the energies that surround you. When making your talisman, as with all other aspects of your gris gris bag, consider your intention.

We like using woods that carry particular properties. A talisman can be as simple as binding two small pieces of white ash together with leather in a cross shape, which is one of the most universal symbols of power and intention. A circle, which indicates an eternal commitment or unending life, can be fashioned by twisting a sprig of fresh willow and allowing it to dry. Within it, a natural thread could be woven in the image of a pentagram or to indicate the points of the four winds. Small pieces of birch may be burned (with a simple wood-burning kit) with the images of runes, the ankh, a pentagram, astrological signs, or any number of magical symbols. You may also incorporate numerology, tarot symbols, or personal drawings—anything that will satisfy your relationship to the bag. Small pieces of different woods may also be bundled together to bring forth the innate magic of several different trees.

Items you find in your memory box—broken costume jewelry, a wooden clothespin, or other things that connect you to your ancestry—may also be used as a talisman. You may use a piece of fur from your favorite pet, or a whisker, claw, or feather (naturally shed of course) to create an even more personal connection. Then add painted symbols, sprigs of dried herbs, or a piece of ribbon to make the bag completely your own.

part three

Spells

INTENTION & FOCUS

· · · · · · · · · · · · · · · ·

A spell is simply the focused working of magic. In the act of assembling your gris gris bag, you are casting a spell. Intention is always the key, of course, but another vital element for your spell's success (your bag's success) is specificity. If you create a bag for love, you must decide if you want to feel true love, or to have someone love you, or whether you're simply seeking more passion in an existing relationship. Also, you'll want to call for true love to enter your life in a fair exchange, or you may be inviting in the pain of unrequited adoration. Also be sure to consider any repercussions of your desires; you shouldn't wish for a generic peace, for example, unless you recognize the price of peace (is justice compromised?). In this world of balances, a payment is due on everything.

Once you have thoughtfully considered your intention for your bag and any consequences of your desires, you are ready to begin the process. In the following pages, we've listed spells for many situations, and included suggestions for everything from bag color to types of stones and herbs, to the timing of the spell, to incantations for expressing your intent. One thing to remember when reading these spells is that the incantations we offer are optional. We designed the chants as strategic rhymes to aid you with concentration; incantations are like prayers in that way. But you can certainly choose to write your own incantations to express your intent, and indeed, many of the spells in this book leave the nature of the chant up to you. When writing your own chants, feel free to borrow from a classic work or create your own phrases, using a rhyme involving an intended's name or the name of a job position you want, for instance.

Whatever words you use, we recommend stating and repeating your intention from the moment you begin gathering your ingredients—choosing your bag color, measuring your herbs, selecting your special objects, etc. For example, you can say, "I add these items with the intention of attracting prosperity." You may use this (or a related) chant during the actual assembly of the bag, and it's a good idea to repeat the chant once the bag is complete: "I have added these items together with the intention of attracting prosperity." We suggest holding the finished bag in your left hand and repeating the intent/chant three times, to seal the deal.

Keep in mind, however, that it is not necessary to state your intention out loud. Some people find they're more focused if they remain silent. The act of assembling the bag, rather than the words per se, is the most significant part of the spell. Choosing not to chant or use spell words does not lessen the effectiveness of the bag. You may prefer to listen to music, or to assemble the bag outside to be closer to nature. While chants can help your focus, they are not essential elements—it is a personal choice.

Whatever your approach, be sure to remain focused and specific and do not allow for disturbances during the spell process. We recommend doing spell work late at night, when electricity use is down and ambient noise is at a minimum. The sounds of nature are always acceptable. And try to assemble your bag without artificial breezes, such as those from fans or air conditioners.

SPELLS FOR LOVE
· · · · · · · · · · · · · · ·

The quest for love has always been one of the greatest there is. We all wish to have someone to share our lives with, to love us, guard us, and fill our days and nights with passion, companionship, and comfort. Think of the most famous stories ever told, whether the tale of Eros in Greek mythology, Shakespeare's tragedy *Romeo and Juliet*, or Jane Austen's *Pride and Prejudice*. People get dopamine rushes just from watching other people in love. The very idea of everlasting love fills our hearts with hope, no matter how difficult our own lives may seem.

Love is a commanding drug. It can overtake the body, mind, and spirit, and lead us to change the entire course of our life with its simple promise. It flows through us with a pulsing commitment to tomorrow, and can breathe life into even the most cynical pessimist. Scientifically, love releases chemicals in our brain that cause us to feel giddy and euphoric; not even the handy substitute, chocolate, can sate our soul's craving for the real thing. So why wouldn't we want to attract love into our lives?

The following spells are for bags that not only attract love, but also encourage its growth (engagement), maintain it (fidelity and good marriage), and stoke its fires (passion). If you seek to remove a toxic relationship from your life, we recommend the Spell for Good Riddance located in Spells for Healing section.

We must caution you, however, to always be careful with what you wish for when it comes to focusing on specific people and love. Sometimes the person we think we desire turns out to be the wrong one for us. Always step back and allow the universe to manifest its wisdom. In our experience, the more willing you are to give love, the more readily it shall be returned to you; we don't recommend trying to bend the will of another person toward love. Just to be on the safe side, it is far better to ask for love to visit in a general sense—love comes in many forms.

If you choose to use words while assembling your spell bag, consider the qualities you seek in your proposed lover. You can write your own chant easily by asking for guidance from the universe. Imagine yourself holding hands and enjoying that familiar, wonderful feeling of being fully connected to another person. Try to get a sense of your lover's individuality, and of the positive, comforting, and supportive energy that will bind with yours and help you to flourish.

As mentioned above, a piece of classic poetry can serve this purpose well. Two wonderful poems to consider are Elizabeth Barrett Browning's Sonnet 43, which begins, "How do I love thee? Let me count the ways," and Shakespeare's Sonnet 18, which begins, "Shall I compare thee to a summer's day?"

For Attracting Love

There are so many herbs and stones to choose from for this bag, you might just select the ones you think look the loveliest. Remember to use the lists in these spells only as guidelines—let the objects you collect speak to you directly. After all, this love gris gris bag is yours and yours alone, and should be placed where you will see it, smell its aroma, and remember that love is coming. Do not let anyone else, your love interest included, touch your gris gris bag (you may remember listening to blues songs such as Coot Grant and Wesley "Kid Sox" Wilson's "Keep Your Hand Off My Mojo"; they knew what they were talking about). And always remember to keep the total number of items in your bag an odd number.

Bag Color:
Pink

Plants:
Acorn, anise, apple, basil, black cohosh, bloodroot, caraway seeds, catnip, cedar, cinnamon, cinquefoil, cloves, dandelion, fig, ginger, ginseng, ivy, jasmine, lavender, lemon verbena, linden, lovage, mandrake, marigold, marjoram, mistletoe, myrtle, nutmeg, olive, orange (can inscribe the person's name on the peel), pine, primrose, rosemary, roses, rowan, rue, saffron, St. John's wort, valerian, vervain, willow, yarrow

Stones, Metals, and Shells:

Copper, emerald, lodestone, magnetic sand, malachite, pink coral, pink tourmaline, rose quartz, selenite

Other Items:

A lock of hair or a fingernail clipping from the other person should be included if possible. Ashes, heart tokens, and other love talismans are good additions to the bag, and they increase the power of the spell. The addition of a feather will speed the love to you.

Candle Color:

Pink

Day of the Week:

Friday

Calendar:

Waxing or full moon

Special Instructions:

If you are asking your gris gris bag to attract a specific person to you, keep a photograph of that person in your sacred space and focus on good thoughts and a positive outcome while gazing at the photo. (In other words, while you should not bend the will of someone who is genuinely not interested in you, a carefully constructed love spell can remove obstacles and open up possibilities. Stating that you're willing to accept an outcome that is best for all concerned is a good way to hedge your bets.) You may also wish to write the person's name on a slip of paper beforehand, fold the paper, and include it in the bag. Likewise, you can burn the paper in the candle flame after the bag has been created, visualizing the future love you will share. You may anoint your bag with rose oil every week to enhance its energy.

Chant:

Here is a simple chant we like to use when seeking a true and lasting love or soul mate. It is written to acknowledge that if love is meant to be, then no distance, whether physical or spiritual, will keep two destined lovers apart. You may substitute "she" for "he" if so desired.

Two beating hearts on distant shores
With full intent, I open doors
I traverse waves, if there be need
And scale the mountain to plant the seed
Upon this earth, my true love dwells
With ancient truth, my passion swells
With fervent will, I call to thee
To light the path, from he to me
When meet our eyes, the truth be known
And fill our spirits, blood and bone
Then joined in love, forever be
Two hearts as one, me to he.

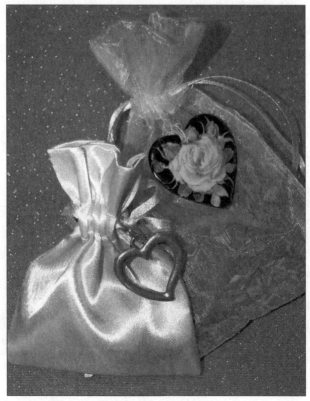

Gris gris bags for attracting love.

For Engagement

In Romanian tradition, a girl will present her loved one with basil to signify their engagement. In Europe and America, apples and nuts were used in a number of Halloween charms in the hopes of revealing who was going to marry whom. The gris gris bag described below should be used primarily to entice your loved one to pop the question.

Bag Color:
Pink

Plants:
Basil, birch, elder flowers, lavender, lovage, rosemary

Stones:
Amber, bloodstone, fire citrine, sapphire

Other Items:
A lock of hair or a fingernail clipping from each person. Also, the bride and groom figurines that top wedding cakes, or wedding ring tokens found at wedding suppliers, or puzzle pieces that join together to signify the union of two souls.

Candle Color:
Green

Day of the Week:
Thursday

Calendar:
Waxing or full moon

For Fidelity

In the voodoo tradition, women would visit the priestess and request gris gris bags to quell their man's potentially roving eye. The priestess often gave the women instructions for other measures to prevent roving—such spells, called "binding spells," often involved bodily fluids, like semen or menstrual fluid, surreptitiously added to a sauce and ingested by an unsuspecting lover or spouse. We don't recommend anything so drastic, but suggest including items in your bag that place both you and your lover together in a positive light, one that reflects loyalty and fidelity.

Nutmeg is a good spice of choice for fidelity bags, which are then put beneath your partner's pillow to help ensure that he or she doesn't roam. But if you are interested in adding something to your cooking to keep your partner at home, try marjoram. When cooked in a favorite dish, marjoram strengthens love.

As you construct your fidelity bag, allow the energies of the herbs, stones, and other objects you collect to suggest which combinations will work best for your specific situation. When tallying your total number of items, remember to allow for personal elements (hair, fingernail clipping) to be added.

Bag Color:
Brown

Plants:
Basil, caraway seeds, cinnamon, elder, marigold, marjoram, mistletoe, nutmeg, orange, pine needles, rosemary

Stones:
Beryl, jade (Egyptians thought jade preserved love), lapis lazuli, lodestone, rose quartz, sapphire

Other Items:
A lock of hair, a piece of clothing, or a fingernail clipping from each person. Tokens such as rings or hearts make for good ingredients as well. A photo of the one you love can be placed by the candle so you can view it as you create.

Candle Color:
Brown or pink

Day of the Week:
Monday

Calendar:

Waxing or full moon

Chant:

If you had special vows at your marriage ceremony and still have them written down somewhere, you could recite them while assembling your bag. The following words may be recited as well:

> *A lock of hair*
> *A vision of you*
> *To bind our love*
> *And make it true*
> *Be close, my love*
> *And see us through*
> *Unite our souls*
> *Of me, of you*

For Friendship

People who have moved to new towns or taken on a new job may want to enlist the help of certain herbs and stones to make new friends. (And if you should feel the need for a protection gris gris, the stones magnesite and nephrite can help protect you against potentially false friends.)

Bag Color:

Pink

Plants:

Mandrake, passionflower

Stones:

Diamond, jade, rose quartz, turquoise

Candle Color:

Pink

Day of the Week:
Saturday

Calendar:
Waxing moon

Chant:
A simple chant would be:

> *Ease my loneliness with this spell, bring me friends*
> *and wish us well.*

For something more complex, you might try:

> *Guide me as I walk this path*
> *New to me and new to them*
> *Turn the tides of lonely lack*
> *And help me to begin again*
> *Open up all hearts and minds*
> *Find our equal, common ground*
> *Initiate new ties that bind*
> *Fill my life with friendships found*

For a Good Marriage

If you're creating this bag for yourself, you should have a photo of the two of you together. If you're already married, a wedding photo works best. If you wish to give the gris gris bag to a couple as a wedding present, you may want to glue or sew a small photo of the couple on the outside of the bag and tie it closed with a white ribbon or string. Some of the ingredients to consider are birch bark (when people jumped the broom in olden days, it was usually a birch broom), and lavender and rosemary for their deliciously pungent, loving scent. Rice, which has been affiliated with weddings since the time of the Assyrians and ancient Egyptians, promises fertility and a bountiful life.

Bag Color:
White or brown

Plants:

Anise, apple, birch, ivy, lavender, lovage, magnolia, marjoram, orange, pine, rice, rosemary

Stones:

Rose quartz

Other Items:

A lock of hair, or fingernail clippings from you and your partner. If this is a wedding present, explain to the couple that adding something personal from each of them is essential for charging the bag with their energy.

Candle Color:

White or brown

Day of the Week:

Monday

Calendar:

Waxing or full moon

Chant:

> *We said our vows*
> *We merged our love*
> *Bring blessings upon us*
> *From spirits above*
> *May our love blossom*
> *As in all things vernal*
> *Keep us safe,*
> *Our love eternal.*

For Passion

This gris gris bag for passion can serve two different purposes. It can restore passion in relationships that could use a jolt of heat, or help relationships that have sexual dysfunctions. Whatever the reason you choose to create the passion gris gris, be mindful of the fiery elements assembled here: spicy herbs such as black pepper, cayenne, and ginger, and stones like fire agate and fire opal. You can hang the bag from your bedpost or place it beneath the bed to ensure, enhance, or aid sexual passion.

Bag Color:
Red

Plants:
Black pepper, bloodroot, cayenne, cinnamon, (red) clover, date palm, dill, fenugreek, ginger, horse nettle, nettle, palmetto, rosemary, roses, saffron

Stones:
Amber, carnelian, fire agate, fire opal, garnet, red aventurine, ruby, staurolite, vanadinite

Candle Color:
Red

Day of the Week:
Tuesday

Calendar:
Waxing or full moon

Passion gris gris bags.

Chant:

When creating your chant, be sure to use active words filled with the passion you hope to create. Feel the heat as you recite, and let the same energy you hope to manifest become part of the whole process, start to finish. Here is a suggested chant:

> *With fire of truth, red and real*
> *Help my lover, strong to feel*
> *Bring about the flame aglow*
> *Fall within passion's flow*
> *Heat shall burn through mouth and heart*
> *Fill our loins with fever's spark*
> *And tie us in a tangled rage*
> *Knotted in a lover's cage*
> *With lover's sweat, we both are drenched*
> *When sated, shall we both be quenched*
> *Our nestled forms then intertwined*
> *With body, spirit, heart. and mind.*

For Removing Toxic Relationships

See *For Good Riddance* in the **Spells for Healing** section.

SPELLS FOR PROSPERITY

· · · · · · · · · · · · · · · ·

Like so many of you, we long for prosperity, good fortune, and for all our wishes to come true. Both of us have everyday needs that must be met. For example, our kids are headed off to college, our cars need repair, and our homes are calling out for renovation. All of these issues prompted the question: can one be minutely specific about a prosperity wish? The answer is a resounding *Yes!* The idea of specificity of intent when creating a gris gris is not so different from the "law of attraction" discussed earlier; in fact, the more specific your intent, the better.

Many of the spells in this section show you how to achieve overall prosperity, but we've added individual spells for specific purposes such as finding employment or prevailing in court. We've also included a gris gris bag designed uniquely for home improvement needs. This may be reaching a bit out of the box (or rather, the bag), but that's what we're used to.

A prosperity gris gris bag.

For example, Cheré badly needed a new bathroom. Water damage had made the repairs costly and the room needed to be completely gutted. She saw a photo in a magazine of the exact shower she wanted, so she cut it out and placed the photo inside a three-inch cloth bag. Then she hunted around for a photo of the right faucets and other fixtures, plus obtained a sample tile and a paint color chip she thought would be perfect. By the time Cheré had her whole bathroom designed and planned, she had collected five items for her bag. She combined them with a dash of cinquefoil and High John the Conqueror, and now has a bathroom-renovation gris gris hanging from her shower. She knows that the renovation is on the way.

The moral of this story is that you don't have to stick to the plants, stones, and other items listed for these spells. Household objects or color samples, as well as photographs, are the best items for these gris gris bags, especially if your need is very specific. If you're looking for funds to create a new garden, for instance, a collection of seeds in your gris gris may fit the bill. Or if you'd like to find the resources to install solar heating, then, by all means, include a small photograph of solar panels. As long as your intentions do no harm, the possibilities are endless.

For Attracting Prosperity

On January first, Southerners enjoy Hoppin' John, a dish of black-eyed peas, and greens (kale, chard, mustard greens, turnip greens), in the belief that this will attract prosperity in the coming year. The greens match the color of money and the peas resemble coins, and a hot slice of cornbread makes it all taste good together. Southern sayings for New Year's Day include, "Peas for pennies, greens for dollars, and cornbread for gold," and "Eat poor on New Year, and eat fat the rest of the year."

You can use these same ideas when creating a prosperity gris gris bag. Items to put in your bag that resemble money include large basil leaves, black-eyed peas, dill seeds, mojo beans, and pecans, and of course you can add green stones such as emeralds, green aventurine, green jade, or malachite.

Bag Color:
Green

Plants:
Angelica root, ash, basil, bay laurel, birch, blackberry, black-eyed peas, camellia, cedar, chamomile, cinquefoil, four-leaf and five-leaf clover, cloves, comfrey, dandelion, dill seeds, echinacea, fenugreek, ferns, fig, ginger, gold, High John the Conqueror root, lucky hand root, mandrake, mint, mojo beans, moss, myrtle, nutmeg, oak, orange, palm, pecan, pine, rice, sage, vervain

Stones, Metals, and Shells:
Citrine, clam shell, emerald, garnet, green aventurine, green jade, green tourmaline, gold, lodestone, opal, magnetic sand, malachite, peridot, pyrite, ruby, sand dollar, staurolite, tiger's eye, vanadinite

Other Items:
Coins, dollar bills, magnet, a mirror, a silver dollar

Candle:
Green

Day of the Week:
Thursday

Calendar:
Waxing or full moon

Special Instructions:
Like good fortune, the idea of prosperity can be vague. We each have our own idea of what constitutes prosperity. Also, prosperity can be a catch-all, encompassing wealth, success, and good fortune. But as we've mentioned before, specificity can infuse your intention with energy. Be clear on what prosperity means to you as you create

your bag. Imagine, in your world, how your success will manifest and be recognized, and embrace the feelings that will come with it.

For Business Success

Often we will enter a store and see a framed dollar bill behind the counter. It's common practice for a fledgling business to save their first dollar as a good luck omen and display it proudly. Creating a gris gris bag for business success draws from the same type of belief: from the first there shall be many.

The best way to attract wealth and success to a business is to combine your first dollar earned (or a recent dollar that has meaning) with magnetic sand, lucky hand root, and a lodestone. Together in a bag, these magical ingredients will work to multiply that one dollar and create success. Chinese coins also work well. And if you want to use something as simple as a silver dollar or dime, success will be yours as long as you ask for it. Another option is to use old money. An extremely worn, well-handled coin of any denomination can bring with it the promise of gain. The theory behind this is that the coin has been infused with the understanding of value and exchange through its repeated handling, and the core metals, especially silver, used in older coins are great for absorbing and transferring energy.

Bag Color:
Green

Plants:
Basil, devil's shoestring, High John the Conqueror root, lucky hand root, nutmeg

Stones, Metals, and Shells:
Carnelian, cowrie shells, lodestone, magnetic sand, malachite

Other Items:
Dollar bills, Chinese coins, silver coins

168 · *Part Three*

Candle Color:
Green

Day of the Week:
Thursday

Calendar:
Waxing or full moon

Chant:
When devising a chant to accompany spells for prosperity and success in business, remember to recognize the importance of the extended consequences of your intention. If you include a consequence (for example, wishing that success in your jewelry store business will bring happiness to all the couples buying engagement rings from you), it will add a little punch to your work. Here's a simple suggestion:

> *As my efforts fill my coffers,*
> *May they fill the hearts of many.*

For Gaining Employment

Before you assemble your bag, imagine the perfect job and visualize yourself being part of that business. Ask the universal spirits to grant you the position as you create your gris gris, always asking for blessings, protection, and divine wisdom. As with love spells, looking for the perfect job takes a lot of consideration. If you know of a specific company where you'd like to work, take the time to research them and make sure it's a good fit. Sometimes what appears ideal on the surface can be a disappointment when it comes to the nine-to-five grind. And always remember, no gris gris spell works without translating your intention into physical effort. You do have to take action—go out, look for the job, and apply.

Bag Color:
Green

Plants:
Basil, devil's shoestring, lucky hand root, parsley

Stones and Metals:
Carnelian, magnetic sand

Other Items:
The want ad for the position you seek

Candle Color:
Green

Day of the Week:
Thursday

Calendar:
New moon

Special Instructions:
Carry the gris gris bag (carefully hidden, of course) with you to job interviews. Also, as with the Business Success spell chant, take a moment to consider the far-reaching ramifications of acquiring the position. Think about the people you can help with your newfound influence. Also, remember to view small failures as nothing more than a change in direction guided by a loving universe, and remain confident that your reward is coming.

For Good Fortune

There are many symbols, icons, talismans, and unique natural objects that we adopt to ensure good fortune. Everything from a lucky rabbit's foot to a four-leaf clover have given people that extra sense of security as they make their way through the day. Of course, good luck is an indefinable concept. It's as individual as we are, and usually takes our personal history, ethnic background, religious beliefs, and geographical location into account. When creating a gris gris bag for good luck, all of the above is allowable. Your gris gris is your personal message to the universe, a call for a connection, to combine your powers (intention) with those of a greater power and make your wishes come true.

The idea of good fortune can be vague, but as long as you have clarity in your intention, it shouldn't matter. Add any one of your favorite good fortune tokens to your bag to truly make it your own. Another suggestion is to mix coral, turquoise, and amber, strong in different ways alone but powerful in good fortune together. The Chinese "three fortunate fruits"—citron, peach, and pomegranate—symbolize abundance and plenty, and may be included as well. Their sweetness, rich flavors, and medicinal properties are offerings to the gods when seeking good fortune. The pomegranate enfolds hundreds of seeds protected within a tough exterior, a clear symbol of security and abundance; the peach's fleshy sweetness indicates a flavorful life; and citron has long been used to protect against illness. These fruits may be dried or powdered to add to the bags, or dried slices can be bundled and used as a talisman on the bag's exterior. Tokens representing these three fruits work just as well as the real thing.

Bag Color:
Gold

Plants:
Basil, buckeyes, cedar, cinquefoil, elder leaves and berries, holly leaves, linden, pine

Stones, Metals, and Shells:
Citrine, lodestone, magnetic sand, sand dollar

Other Items:
Any type of good-fortune symbol, a fortune from a fortune cookie

Candle Color:
Gold

Day of the Week:
Sunday

Calendar:

Waxing or full moon

Special Instructions:

Carry the bag with you at all times, and have an extra to keep by your bed or under your pillow. You can even make a bag for each member of your household. If you make bags for your family, have each include an individual good luck charm of their own.

For Luck in Court

Over the years, mojo and gris gris bags have drawn on a number of unusual herbs to help their wearer win in court. Black mustard seeds and black poppy seeds are said to cause confusion for the opposing party, especially if the opposing party is the accuser. Slippery elm protects the wearer in court, particularly against false testimony and slander, and calendula blossoms and cinquefoil help ensure victory. A whole galangal root (a member of the ginger family) has a long history of protecting its wearer from harm in court. Ginger can also prove effective for success, especially in money matters.

Bag Color:

Green

Plants:

Black mustard seeds, black poppy seeds, calendula, chestnuts, cinquefoil, hickory nuts, galangal, High John the Conqueror root, Low John the Conqueror, slippery elm, ginger

Stones and Shells:

Amethyst, bloodstone, hematite, lodestone, malachite, scallop shells

Other Items:

Justice tarot card, Michael the Archangel card, shark's tooth

Candle Color:

Green

Day of the Week:
Thursday

Calendar:
Waxing or full moon

Special Instructions:
The bag should be kept with you in court and during any prior and later proceedings. Keep it with you when you draft correspondence regarding the court case, and definitely when signing any legal documents.

For Luck in Gambling

Gamblers are by nature superstitious, believing that any number of peculiar items or actions will help them win the day. If you have a particular item you believe brings you luck at the gaming tables or horse track, by all means use it. But if you need suggestions, we have plenty listed. A typical New Orleans luck-in-gambling gris gris bag would be green and contain High John the Conqueror root, cinquefoil, lucky hand root, dice, lodestone, a coin, and a cowrie shell.

Bag Color:
Green

Plants:
Angelica, devil's shoestring, five-finger grass, High John the Conqueror root, lucky hand root, rue

Stones, Metals, and Shells:
Green aventurine, lodestone, magnetic sand, sand dollar, yellow and purple cowrie shells

Other Items:
Dice, coins, gambling chips, lottery tickets, lucky number written on paper, rabbit's foot, racing form, silver dollar, Wheel of Fortune tarot card

Candle Color:
Green

Day of the Week:
Thursday

Calendar:
Waxing or full moon

Special Instructions:
Part of winning has to do with mental attitude. Have you ever heard a friend say, "If it wasn't for bad luck, I'd have no luck at all?" Their misfortune is inevitable. When you're building your luck-in-gambling gris gris bag, you should banish all thoughts of failure. Repeat in your mind how happy you are that things are going so well for you, and imagine that great feeling of having garnered your winnings. With this kind of energy filling the bag, connected to all the other items, winning is just a wish away.

For Lottery Tickets

To create this bag, use some of the same ingredients as in the luck-in-gambling bag. If you have specific numbers that you like to play, especially printed on a former lottery ticket, place that in the bag as well.

Bag Color:
Green

Plants:
Angelica root, basil, four-leaf and five-leaf clover, High John the Conqueror root, mojo beans

Stones and Shells:
Citrine, green aventurine, green jade, lodestone, sand dollar

Other Items:
Coins, lucky numbers written on a piece of paper

Candle Color:
Green

Day of the Week:
Thursday

Calendar:
Waxing or full moon

Special Instructions:
As when doing other spells, consider adding a couple of protection elements to your intention; you'll want to guard against "the curse of the lottery." Whether this curse is true or not depends on the individual—every day people win lotteries and experience no problems, but the larger jackpots have frequently ushered disaster into the lives of the winners. As you build your bag, ask for guidance and wisdom as well as protection from greed. Say that you don't want to lose your way because of the monumental financial change in your life, and always consider sharing your winnings.

For Wishes

We don't believe that wishes should be kept secret. Be vocal about your desires. Write them down, say them aloud, scream them if you feel you should. Tell them to the heavens and let the world know your intentions. This can be as simple as writing a wish on a piece of paper, folding it tightly, and placing it in your bag. Or you can add some punch by writing it on a sage, bay, or fig leaf, or upon the skin of ginger root—the natural energy in the plant will help bring your wish to fruition. Combine this wish with a few select herbs and flowers, a stone, and perhaps a spiral of copper wire for conductive energy, and your intention should manifest.

Bag Color:
Green

Plants:
Dandelion, ginger, ginseng, hazel, sage, sunflower

Stones and Metals:
Copper wire, smoky quartz

Candle Color:
Green

Day of the Week:
Thursday

Calendar:
Waxing or full moon

Special Instructions:
Be careful what you wish for—this simple statement carries a lot of meaning. When you are truly ready to pursue your desires, really consider everything that could come with them. Consider how your wish will affect others, and never wish for pain or injury to another. As with every effort we make in the magical world, the law of three applies. That which you cast out shall return to you threefold. Or as Jude's dad used to say, "Always make your words sweet, in case you have to eat them."

SPELLS FOR HEALING
. . . .

Many people think of health as the mere absence of illness. Only recently have we begun to consider overall well-being as essential to physical health. We now know that we should seek to achieve an inclusive balance within ourselves, with other people, within nature, and within our surroundings. As is the case with all natural things, the energy that flows through our bodies can become hampered by blockages due to stress, anger, failure to forgive, emotional trauma, and other ailments "beyond" our bodies that we neglect to acknowledge. An exercise in healing needs to encompass all key aspects of the self: physical, emotional, mental, and spiritual. We must enter into healing with an open mind and a certain fearlessness, as we take a hard look at what might be the root cause of our maladies.

Pain can result from something as simple as not sitting properly while working on a computer. This can cause cramped shoulder muscles, knots in the neck, headache, back problems, carpal tunnel syndrome, and even stomach discomfort. But the reason for bad posture stems from our not paying attention to our body as it signals us with the pain. We're too quick to treat symptoms, rather than investigate the underlying causes of an issue. Striving to achieve balance throughout the day, in the four key aspects of the self, should become a goal for everyone. You'd be surprised at how many ailments can be avoided with just a simple shift in consciousness.

A healing gris gris bag enlists the assistance of nature's best elements to bring the body back to center and achieve harmony and balance in our lives. Gris gris is not meant to cure illness or to take the place of a physician or wellness practitioner, but rather to assist us in self-awareness and self-improvement, addressing the areas that are often overlooked by conventional medicine.

When doing a healing gris gris spell, it's always best to create your own bag. Only you know what you seek when it comes to a specific discomfort. (Imagine trying to explain all aspects of your problem to a physician; it's nearly impossible to convey through words how you're feeling, and then it's left up to the physician to not only interpret your description, but to decipher the cause of an ailment explained in layman's terms.) However, if you wish to help someone in pain who cannot make their own bag, or give a bag as a token of kindness, go ahead and do so—better yet, perhaps work on the bag together. Using a photo of your friend while making the bag is helpful; focus on the person and the banishment of their discomfort or ailment.

As always, it's imperative to cleanse your sacred space by burning purifying herbs such as cedar, sage, and juniper, or using a birch broom to ceremoniously brush away the negativity in the area. Banishing negativity from your life may also bring peace and balance, thus curing you of an illness. Consider creating a gris gris bag to promote peace, endurance, courage, etc. Also, the Spell for Good Riddance can be an effective way to banish specific illness from your life.

For Calming & Stress Relief

This may sound like something you've heard in yoga class, but deep breathing and/or meditation works wonders for this spell. If nothing else, it will put you in the right frame of mind. Focus on your breath as you breathe in and out, the exhale longer than the inhale, and visualize yourself completely at peace. Imagine a white light surrounding your sacred space and your bag. (This white light methodology can work in so many areas of your life. Try it sometime if you're feeling overwhelmed at home or at work. It only takes a few minutes, but the results are amazing.) Once you feel rejuvenated, get to work at creating your calming bag.

Bag Color:
Blue

Plants:
Chamomile, lavender, passionflower, valerian, vervain

Stones:

Amber, blue quartz, blue tourmaline, celestite (which, if not placed in the bag, is great to have on hand during the bag's preparation), kunzite, lapis lazuli, moss agate, pink calcite

Candle:

Blue

Day of the Week:

Sunday

Calendar:

Waning moon to banish stress, waxing moon to bring in peace

Special Instructions:

There are many stones associated with stress relief. Consider wearing your favorite relaxation crystal, or just keep it on hand while assembling your bag. Keep in mind that creating a peaceful, undisturbed environment is essential while building a stress-release bag. What you're feeling inside invariably infuses your efforts. It wouldn't hurt to turn off your phone, TV, radio, and computer and disconnect yourself from outside influences. Be selfish with abandon. This should be exclusively your time, because you've earned it.

Chant:

> Peace be with me.
> Peace be with all.

For Cancer (and other diseases)

We cannot stress enough that gris gris bags are no substitute for traditional treatments and cures for cancer or other diseases, so please see your physician or wellness practitioner in addition to making this bag. That said, it is important to recognize that we are not victims of our disease. Studies have repeatedly shown that stress can bring about any number of problems, just as a physical phenomenon like exposure to chemicals does (whether the chemicals are in the atmosphere, absorbed through the skin, or ingested through foods). Likewise, smoking is a huge problem for many people because of its addictive properties and the level of damage it can do to the body. Last but not least, poor eating habits plague much of our nation, even when healthy alternatives are readily available.

The first step to healing is to honor your body. Each individual is a whole being, inextricably connected in a physical/spiritual symbiosis. If how we feel (stress) can affect us physically, then how we behave physically (poor habits) can affect us spiritually. And spiritual imbalance can have far-reaching effects on every other aspect of our lives. Take the time to reevaluate your lifestyle as you seek to improve your overall health. Look for areas where you can initiate conscious change to help put yourself on the road to wellness.

This cancer/illness gris gris bag is designed to invoke the healing spirits of its ingredients and to help you visualize the tumor or disease leaving your body while balance, harmony, and joy take its place. An ideal bag for cancer would contain rosemary, thyme, dill, mint, and parsley, because of their inherent cancer-fighting properties.

Bag Color:
Blue or green

Plants:
Angelica, bay leaves, cinnamon, dill, fennel seeds, garlic, High John the Conqueror root, horsehound, mint, parsley, rose, rosemary, thyme, vervain, yew

Stones:
Agate, amber, black tourmaline, bloodstone

Special Instructions:
Write the name of the affliction in blue ink on a piece of paper, then draw a large X through it indicating that it must be removed from your body. Burn the paper and place the ashes into your bag. This type of ritual is the first step to recognizing your power over

the disease. It helps if you state that the malady is not welcome in your body, that it does not belong to you and it must move on.

Candle Color:
Green

Day of the Week:
Sunday

Calendar:
Waning moon

Chant:

> *Disease and illness take flight*
> *Replace darkness with divine light.*

For Colds & Flu

Nothing is more appropriately named than the common cold. We all seem to get one at least once a year. Many herbs are enlisted in the fight against colds and flu—our mothers' recipes included everything from gargling with salt water to drizzling honey down our throats to ease pain and congestion. The smell of eucalyptus and camphor are familiar ingredients found in Vick's VapoRub and other aids for sore muscles, congestion, and body aches. Many over-the-counter medicines contain herbal extracts that ease our pain. In Louisiana, small amounts of the root of the mamou plant, or eastern coral bean, serve as an expectorant, and mamou seeds depress the nerves to help ease coughs. If you have access to this plant, definitely add its seeds to the bag.

Colds are funny things. They may seem like a nuisance, but often they're nature's way of telling us to slow down. We're most susceptible to colds when our resistance is compromised. We may be run-down, suffering from internal struggles, not taking good care of ourselves, or just pushing ourselves to the limit. Colds, while definitely annoying, force us to take stock, evaluate our recent behaviors, and, most importantly, learn to say "No." A cold is our body's way of reminding us that rest is essential, both physically and spiritually. Close off the world, have some hot ginger tea with honey, and relax.

Keep your colds-and-flu gris gris bag on hand to remind yourself that your health is paramount, even among the pressing priorities of your busy schedule.

Bag Color:
Orange

Plants:
Bergamot, cayenne, elder, eucalyptus, feverfew (for fever), garlic, ginger, holly, mamou, sage, St. John's wort

Stones:
Agate, bloodstone, jet, red jasper (for fever), sulfur, zircon

Other Items:
A hot toddy (hot tea with a shot of whiskey or brandy, honey, and lemon juice) is a sure-fire way to ease a cold and help one sleep. If you indulge in one while you make this bag, we won't tell.

Candle Color:
Orange

Day of the Week:
Sunday

Calendar:
Waning moon

Chant:
Let your chant be a simple one—wish wellness for the world.

For Digestive Problems

The positive effects of a nice cup of chamomile or mint tea on digestion are well proven. We can't help but sing their praises. They're simple remedies for a simple malady. More serious digestive problems require more than a cup of tea, of course, and again, always consult with your doctor or health practitioner.

Try sipping a cup of chamomile tea while making this gris gris bag. If nothing else, the agreeable scent will put you in the right frame of mind.

Bag Color:
Orange or yellow

Plants:
Cayenne, chamomile, dill, fenugreek, ginger, lemon verbena, mint, pennyroyal, primrose, saffron, watercress

Stones:
Apache tears, citrine, green jasper, tourmaline, turquoise

Candle Color:
Orange or yellow

Day of the Week:
Sunday

Calendar:
Waning moon

Special Instructions:
As a general rule, always be aware of allergies before drinking any herbal teas or ingesting herbal remedies. If you've never tried herbal medicines before, consult your doctor. Even if you know your allergy history, it's a good idea to try small amounts of anything new first, and ease into a regular regimen.

For General Healing

This gris gris bag doesn't focus on any particular healing or banishment of illness, but rather makes a general appeal for good health and happiness.

Bag Color:
Blue or green

Plants:
Apple, bergamot, blackberry, cinquefoil, crab apple, cypress, eucalyptus, fennel, garlic, ginseng, hyssop, Job's tears, juniper, mandrake, marjoram, mimosa, mistletoe, mugwort, nettle, nutmeg, olive, pine, roses, rowan, rue, saffron, sage, St. John's wort, walnut, willow, witch hazel

Stones and Metals:
Amber, bloodstone, copper, green jade, gold, hematite, jasper, lapis lazuli, petrified wood, red tourmaline, salt

Candle Color:
Blue, green, or white

Day of the Week:
Sunday

Calendar:
Waxing or full moon

Chant:
One of our favorite poems is "No Doctors Today, Thank You" by Ogden Nash. The first two sentences may be recited when creating this bag. They also add a little humor into the mix.

> *They tell me that euphoria is the feeling of feeling*
> *wonderful,*
> *well, today I feel euphorian.*
> *Today I have the agility of a Greek god*
> *and the appetite of a Victorian.*

For Good Riddance

We love to include rue, a pungent and potent evergreen, in this bag because its Greek root, *reuo*, means "to set free." Rue is also an antidote for poison, and therefore the perfect herb to include inside a gris gris bag meant to banish negativity and poison from your life.

Bag Color:
Black

Plants:
Black pepper, cayenne, lotus, rue, sulfur

Stones and Shells:
Barnacles, salt

Candle Color:
Black or white

Day of the Week:
Saturday

Calendar:
Waning moon

Special Instructions:
Always take a positive approach and shape your intentions to be about what is best for you. Using negative energy to wish away problems or people can come back to haunt you. It wouldn't hurt to have a simple protection gris gris on hand as you determine your intention.

Chant:

> *Protect me from those who wish me harm*
> *Encircle this bag with a protective white light*
> *Cast away evil with this charm*
> *Restore balance—absence makes all things right.*

For Headaches

Headaches can be crippling. Even the most minor discomfort can change our mood, inhibit our daily functions, and cause us to retreat from life. It's no surprise that so much research is done on headaches, since relief from headaches is a multibillion-dollar business. But some of the simplest solutions reside in nature—white willow bark was used for centuries to cure headaches, and became the basis for aspirin in the modern world. Feverfew has recently been found to aid in migraine relief, although only when taken at the first signs of a headache. These are some examples of how these age-old herbs remain our friends in the fight against one of the most common and debilitating ailments.

Bag Color:
Blue

Plants:
Feverfew, ginger (makes a great compress as well), lavender, linden, mugwort, rosemary, walnuts, willow

Stones:
Agate, amethyst, celestite, emeralds, hematite, silver, turquoise

Candle Color:
Blue

Day of the Week:
Sunday

Calendar:
Waning moon

Special Instructions:
Visualize your headache pain exiting through the top of your head as positive energy flows up through all seven chakras, beginning with the root chakra at the base of your spine. Hold your gris gris bag in your dominant hand and recite the following.

Chant:

>*I release this pain, negativity, stress, and*
>*imbalance and return to the faultless form of*

*nature. As everything in nature is perfect and
divine, so am I. I am healed. My head is cleared.
I am in perfect harmony with my body and my
spirit.*

For Longevity

In the towns where we grew up, there are massive oak trees believed
to be hundreds of years old. Yew trees are also extremely long-
lived—some are estimated to be two thousand years old—but
yew this old is difficult to find and, of course, yew is quite toxic if
ingested. If handled carefully, both yew and oak make good additions to a longevity gris gris bag. Also effective are ancient stones
such as fossils and petrified wood, and, if you're lucky enough to
have some, the hair of an ancestor.

Bag Color:
Gray

Plants:
Acorns, apple, cypress, nuts, oak, sage, yew

Stones:
Agates, fossils, gold, jade, petrified wood, tiger's eye

Other Items:
An image of the Crone

Candle Color:
Gray

Day of the Week:
Sunday

Calendar:
Waxing or full moon

Chant:

> *Like the mighty trees*
> *Of whose blessings I invoke today*
> *Of ancient stones and fossils*
> *And all who represent longevity*
> *Bestow on me a long life*
> *Through this gris gris bag I pray.*

For Mental Health

There are as many specific afflictions of the mind/brain as there are of the physical body, and mental health issues are not to be taken lightly. When we talk about mental health here, we're referring to the overall wellbeing of your mental state. You can create gris gris bags for yourself, to help find a level place, but keep in mind that it's difficult to create a bag for a friend or loved one who struggles with mental health issues. Sometimes our emotions are too caught up in the process, and there's always an inherent lack of clarity when trying to define the problems of another. Therefore, it's best to create bags for your own purposes, and not to attempt to help others unless it is specifically requested—and in that case, they would need to participate in the bag's creation.

The familiar herb St. John's wort has been used for centuries to combat mild depression. It is widely used today as a key ingredient in many over-the-counter herbal remedies, though it's not sanctioned by modern physicians. For our purposes, we suggest burning it to clear the air of negativity and to cleanse your workspace before creating the bag.

Bag Color:
Pink or white

Plants:
High John the Conqueror root, jasmine, nettles, St. John's wort, thyme

Stones:
Amber, Apache tears, carnelian, fluorite, lapis lazuli, smoky quartz, tiger's eye, zircon

Candle Color:
Black

Day of the Week:
Sunday

Calendar:
Waning moon

Special Instructions:
Write the affliction on paper in blue ink, then burn the paper and place the ashes in the bag to signify the banishment of the disorder.

Chant:

> *Ease my sorrow, ease my mind*
> *Release me from this painful bind*
> *Lift my spirit, wide and free*
> *Help me learn to finally be.*

For Overcoming Difficulties

As mentioned with previous spells, one of the best visualization exercises is to write down your problem on paper, draw an X through it, and burn the paper while reciting, over the ashes (before placing the ashes in your bag), "I am free of your control." Anything that you believe is preventing you from achieving your goals can be written on paper, burned, and included in this spell bag. This ritual is effective as a "casting off" mechanism. You are releasing the malevolent concepts into the universe to be dealt with accordingly, while also releasing your ownership of them.

Bag Color:
Gold

Plants:
Chicory, mojo beans

Stones and Metals:
Citrine, iron, magnetite, onyx, smoky quartz

Other Items:
Objects that represent your struggle or its resolution

Candle:
Gold, white

Day of the Week:
Tuesday

Calendar:
Waning moon

Special Instructions:
If you're experiencing difficulties within a relationship, you may wish to bridge the gap between yourself and the other person. If you're dealing with an unruly teenager, for instance, find a small item or token for your bag that represents a common bond between the two of you. Playing a song you both loved in happier times makes for great ambience when creating this bag, as well. Embrace the positive memories in any way you can, to help shift the energy away from the negative.

For PMS

This may become the most popular gris gris bag among our female readers, and with good reason. Premenstrual syndrome, also known as premenstrual stress syndrome, occurs in nearly ninety percent of women in their childbearing years. It's a familiar experience shared between friends, but remains outside the realm of most males' understanding. It has a long list of symptoms—many similar to menopause—and can manifest as anything from aggressive behavior to swollen breasts and fatigue. The over-the-counter solutions to

PMS number into the dozens. This gris gris bag can help not only as a bag, but through the act of being assembled. Its preparation can offer much needed focus and relaxation for a woman suffering from PMS.

Bag Color:
Blue or green

Plants:
Black cohosh, devil's shoestring, fenugreek, feverfew, ginger, lavender, mugwort, pennyroyal, roses, willow

Stones and Shells:
Bloodstone, celestite, coral, moonstone

Candle:
Blue, green

Day of the Week:
Sunday

Calendar:
Waning moon

Special Instructions:
Clear your space and your mind. Allow yourself some alone-time and totally focus on the task at hand. Feel the balancing energy of the herbs flow through you as you construct your bag, and speak directly to the Goddess, who understands exactly what you're feeling.

Chant:

> *Oh Goddess, Great Mother,*
> *Herbs and stones of the moon,*
> *Bring my body back to balance.*

For Pregnancy & Easy Childbirth

Many of the herbs and stones recommended for this gris gris bag have long histories of helping women during pregnancy and childbirth. Willows and moonstones, for instance, are associated with water and the moon, and therefore are deemed a feminine tree and stone. Black cohosh has long been believed to ease labor cramps (as well as being heavily touted to remedy certain menopausal symptoms), and the Greek physician, pharmacologist, and botanist Dioscorides believed feverfew aided in the contraction of the uterus.

A gris gris bag designed for childbirth can also serve as an effective focal point during labor. Imagine all the energies infused within your bag as you experience the natural wonder of childbirth. The bag can be a familiar companion through the entire pregnancy and a welcome aid as you head to the hospital or birthing center. Please remember, however, to never ingest any herbs during pregnancy unless you first consult with your physician.

Bag Color:
Blue or green

Plants:
Black cohosh, feverfew, roses, willow

Stones and Shells:
Agate, amethyst, bloodstone, coral, geode, jasper, lodestone, moonstone, pumice

Other Items:
A knife token "to cut the pain." (Yes, Prissy in *Gone With the Wind* had the right idea.)

Candle:
Blue, green, white

Day of the Week:
Sunday

Calendar:
Waxing moon

Special Instructions:
Ireland's Brigit is the goddess of midwives and may be invoked for assistance.

For Purification

See *For Cleansing* in the **Spells for Spirituality** section.

For Strength

See the **Spells for Strength & Protection** section.

For Skin Problems

It is a medical fact that skin is the body's largest organ. It is brilliantly designed and serves us in a multitude of ways, but it must be kept clean and free of toxins in order to breathe properly. Unhealthy skin, particularly on the face, can adversely affect a person's self-esteem. If acne is a problem, you may incorporate the following herbs along with those in the Spell for Good Riddance and visualize the banishments of blemishes, pimples, or other skin maladies and the restoration of healthy skin. The more familiar you are with your skin problem, the better your intention will work, so do your homework about what could be causing the condition. Again, you will find that stress is a key factor in skin issues and may manifest in unsightly eruptions. Keep this in mind as you construct your bag. Cleanse your workspace as well as your skin, and start fresh.

Bag Color:
Yellow

Plants:
Comfrey, marigold

Stones:
Amber, carnelian, garnet, sapphires

Candle Color:
Yellow

Day of the Week:
Sunday

Calendar:
Waning moon

Chant:

> *My skin breathes freely,*
> *Glows in harmony*
> *With nature's perfection.*

For Wounds

Wounds are tricky things. Those you expect to last a long time may disappear quickly, while those you consider minor may drag on for days or weeks. It all depends on the true severity, of course, and the cause. It also depends on where you are mentally and spiritually. Cleanse your soul and cleanse the body. Medically, it's very important to keep wounds clean and dry. Also, leave them alone and give your body a chance to catch up. This bag is a great way to help expedite healing while keeping your hands off.

Bag Color:
Blue or green

Plants:
Comfrey, echinachea, juniper, moss, plantain, thyme, vervain, witch hazel, yarrow

Stones and Metals:
Bloodstone, iron, lodestone

Other Items:
Band-aids, staples

Candle Color:
Blue, green, or white

Day of the Week:
Sunday

Calendar:
Waning moon

Chant:

> *Through nature's gifts*
> *My wounds be healed*
> *All illness lifts*
> *And skin be sealed.*

Gris gris bags for healing and overcoming difficulties.

SPELLS FOR FAMILY & HEARTH

. . . .

They are our center, they are our core—they are our family. Family is at the top of nearly everyone's list of priorities. It is within our very nature to preserve the clan, to assist and aid our parents, and to build a safe, protected environment for our children and ourselves. This drive is rooted in our most basic survival instincts. Our offspring receive far greater care and consideration than we give ourselves, and if anything were to threaten the family's survival, it's a sure bet there would be hell to pay.

The following gris gris spells are created to address the basic needs of the family. Whether addressing the safety of children or simple, day-to-day needs, these spells will give you that extra edge as you focus your intention.

For Children

As a parent, your biggest fear is that something bad will happen to your child. It keeps you up at night, drives you to slip into their bedroom to place a mirror beneath their nose, and makes you wait up for all hours until they arrive safely home from a high school party. The greatest gift this gris gris bag can offer is that it helps you focus conscious intention on the protection of your children, rather than play victim to your fears.

Visualize a protective white light surrounding your children as you create this bag, and invoke the spirits you identify with to watch over your children and ease your mind. For a little added security, you can give your children their own protection bags to carry.

Bag Color:
Brown or white

Plants:
Birch, caraway seeds, nutmeg, nuts, primrose, yarrow

Stones and Shells:
Agate, coral, holey stones, lapis lazuli, malachite, moonstone, turquoise

Candle:
Brown, white

Day of the Week:
Tuesday

Calendar:
Waxing moon

Special Instructions:
Early cradles were made of birch wood to protect newborns. Caraway seeds were placed beneath cribs, and nutmeg and yarrow were hung above them for protection. Primrose and cowslip were put inside pillows to make children respect their parents. As with these early methods, your completed gris gris bag may be carried with your child or placed in or around their bed. Although if you have teenagers, all we can say is good luck (we're kidding).

Chant:

> *Goddess of hearth, universal spirits, Mother of*
> *God,*
> *Place your hands on my children's shoulders,*
> *Guide their steps and keep them safe.*
> *Surround them with the universal white light of*
> *protection.*
> *I am like you, a parent, and I bow with gratitude*
> *and offer blessings.*

For Fertility

Even with all the technological advances of modern medicine, some couples still are unable to conceive a child. Throughout history, large families were not only greatly desired, but a necessity; with mortality rates alarmingly high, it was the only way to ensure the continuation of the family name. Today, it is still the greatest gift to be blessed with a healthy child.

Depending on the society, any number of different spells, chants, dances, enlistment of spirits and gods, or other ritual was used to ensure fertility and ask the universe for a bountiful harvest (which is another type of fertility). Specific plants have long histories that relate to fertility rituals, from the apple (or fig, or pomegranate, or quince, depending on your school of thought) that Eve supposedly used to tempt Adam, to the prolific date palm and the mighty oak (with its abundance of acorns). Procreation is one of the most profound ways in which the natural world and human beings truly intersect.

A key consideration when building your fertility gris gris bag is to relax. Take time to let go of the daily tensions that plague your mind and body, and ask nature for her assistance. As you create your bag, know that new life will be created within you. There is no better force to guide procreation than Mother Nature herself.

Bag Color:
Green

Plants:
Acorn, apple, crab apple, date palm, fig, ginseng, hazel, mandrake, mistletoe, myrtle, nutmeg, oak, olive, pine, rice, sunflower, walnut, willow

Stones, Metals, and Shells:
Cowrie shells, geode, magnetic sand, moonstone

Other Items:
Charms from baby showers

Candle Color:
Green

Day of the Week:
Monday

Calendar:

Full moon

Special Instructions:

If the bag is for you, visualize yourself pregnant and healthy, blossoming with the promise of new life. If created for another, visualize her with child.

Chant:

> *I call to you my newborn child*
> *With help from forces here and above*
> *Join with me on this path of life*
> *Open my body to your love.*

For Grieving & Remembrance

There are very few elements available to create this specific bag (as mentioned earlier, you can use as few as three items in your bag, but always an odd number). As a rule, there are two purposes for creating a grieving or remembrance bag: to honor those who have passed through the veil, and to assist us with our grief. You may create a single bag to serve both purposes. If you are calling for the deceased loved one's assistance in helping you cope with your loss, ask for it while making the bag.

Bag Color:

Black

Plants:

Cypress, rosemary, sage

Stones:

Emerald, rose quartz

Other Items:

A piece of the departed's clothing, a lock of their hair, or other small, personal items belonging to the deceased

Candle Color:
Black

Day of the Week:
Saturday

Calendar:
Dark moon

Special Instructions:
As you gather your materials and assemble your bag, place a photo of the departed near the candle and visualize them in a safe, protected place, at peace and joyful.

Chant:
The symbolism of immortality and the happiness of those departed shines in the opening stanza from "There Is No Death" by J. L. McCreery.

> *There is no death! The stars go down*
> *To rise upon some other shore.*
> *And bright in heaven's jeweled crown*
> *They shine forevermore.*

For Hearth & Home

Several years ago, Cheré was considering a job in Birmingham, Alabama. She was attracted to an outlying subdivision, called Vestavia Hills, for its lovely view of the Appalachian foothills. The city was named after the estate of a former mayor who was fascinated with Greco-Roman culture. He was so captivated by the architecture that he had a replica of the ancient Roman temple of Vesta constructed at his estate atop Shades Mountain.

Cheré visited this Greco-Roman temple replica and discovered the story of Vesta, Roman goddess of the hearth and protector of domesticity. In Greek, Vesta's name is Hestia, meaning "fire," and her hearth flames were never allowed to go out. As Zeus' older sister,

Hestia assisted him in controlling chaos in the world. While Cheré didn't end up moving to Birmingham, she was so taken by the story of Vesta that, ever since her children were born, she lights a candle in her hearth in honor of the goddess and asks for intercession in the domestic chaos of everyday life.

A gris gris bag for hearth and home.

We all struggle, every day, to keep our hearth fires lit and chaos under control. When making this gris gris bag, consider enlisting the guidance of Hestia/Vesta as you stoke your spiritual hearth.

Bag Color:
Brown

Plants:
Birch, dandelion, mimosa, pennyroyal

Stones, Metals, and Shells:
Conch shell, iron nail, moonstone

Candle:
Brown

Day of the Week:
Monday

Calendar:
Waxing or full moon

Chant:

> *I sing to you, oh dearest Vesta*
> *Goddess of home, hear my call*
> *Help me keep the hearth fire lit*
> *Shine your light upon us all.*

For a Peaceful Home

Burning sage, cedar smudge sticks, and incense is great for spiritually cleansing a new house or apartment. But when done on a daily basis, it's a wonderful way to help release the air in your home of negativity. So before creating a gris gris bag for a peaceful home, burn sage or a similar cleansing element around your creation space. Also take a few moments and do some deep, meditative breathing to release anxiety and cleanse your body and mind. This will help you achieve a tranquil state, paving the way for visualizations of peace. Find a quiet, calm place in which to connect with these plants and stones as you gather them for your bag, and imagine a worry-free world.

Bag Color:
Brown

Plants:
Angelica root, chamomile, flax seeds, lavender, mimosa, rose

Stones:
Carnelian, malachite, obsidian

Other Items:
Hair from each person in household.

Candle:
Brown

Day of the Week:
Monday

Calendar:
A waxing moon to bring peace into the household. If you are attempting to rid an area of a particularly negative energy, then a waning moon is best.

Chant:

A building made of stick and stone
A spirit housed in blood and bone
Together 'neath the moon and sun
From blessed hour 'til day is done
Protect my home and all who dwell
Bless our paths and guide us well
Banish all who'd do us harm
And keep us safe, secure and warm
May plenty grace our paths and purse
And shelter us from pain and curse
Keep foul intention far at bay
And bless us all with every day.

For Pets

All of us who are pet owners are familiar with the commitment involved in bringing home a four-legged addition to the family. Cheré likes to relate the story of her dear friend Christee Atwood, who welcomed Cheré's family—including three cats and two dogs—when Hurricane Gustav made evacuation necessary. As her mélange of animals howled through the blowing wind and rain, Cheré felt grateful for her pet-loving friend.

Jude, likewise, shares her surprisingly harmonious home with five cats and three dogs, each of whom has a unique personality that brings a different kind of joy to the family. One special addition arrived in the form of a coal-black cat, with vibrant yellow eyes, who appeared in her garage last Halloween. Scarred, scared, and skinny, this gift climbed readily into Jude's arms and melded into the family within just a few days.

Pets are as much a part of our lives as our human family. They offer support, entertainment, stress relief, and most importantly, love and devotion. It's only natural to want to create a gris gris bag to offer protection and good health to these special family members. These bags are also effective for farm animals and animals you may associate with on a daily basis, such as in a zoo or place of employment.

Bag Color:
Brown

Plants:
Black hellebore (for farm animals), catnip and valerian (for cats), anise (for dogs)

Stones:
Rose quartz, holey stones.

Other Items:
Naturally shed fur, whiskers, claws, feathers

Candle Color:
Brown

Day of the Week:
Monday

Calendar:
Waxing or full moon

Chant:
As you add the stones, herbs, and naturally shed items from your pet or farm animal, chant the following three times:

> *Oh spirits, gods, and goddesses,*
> *And the universal light of protection,*
> *Look down upon our family,*
> *And keep them safe from harm.*

For Protection from Accidents

"Accidents happen"—this popular, worn-out phrase is designed to excuse unfortunate events. Occasionally we all have a clumsy day… and then there are those of us who have clumsy years. For those particular times when bumps and bruises become a regular occurrence, you might want to consider this type of gris gris bag. It works best for unfortunate souls such as those mentioned above, or for overall protection when in dangerous places. (You can also combine these ingredients with those used in Safe Travel bags, as added protection for travelers.)

Bag Color:
Brown

Plants:
Feverfew, mistletoe

Stones:
Agate, amber, chalcedony, jade, staurolite

Other Items:
Arrowheads

Candle:
Brown

Day of the Week:
Monday

Calendar:
Waxing or full moon

Special Instructions:
Carry the bag with you at all times. Hold it when you're feeling especially vulnerable.

For Selling a Home

"Never doubt the power of St. Joseph." This is often heard in South Louisiana when people are attempting to sell their home. Catholic residents swear that burying a statue of St. Joseph in your front yard, upside down and facing away from the house, will expedite the sale. We suggest creating a gris gris bag as well. If you do choose to purchase a statue of St. Joseph, keep him near the candle while assembling the bag, then plant him as described in the front yard of the house in question. That way you will gain his influence during the bag's creation and have twice the power of intention. It never hurts to hedge your bets.

Bag Color:
Green

Plants:
Cedar, cinnamon, cloves

Stones:
Carnelian, citrine, lodestone, malachite

Other Items:
St. Joseph's statue, photograph of the home, holy card with St. Joseph

Candle Color:
Green

Day of the Week:
Monday or Thursday

Calendar:
Waxing or full moon

Special Instructions:
While creating the bag, focus on the photograph of the home and visualize a "Sold" sign out front.

Chant:

> *My home calls out to those who seek it.*
> *The right owner shall come forth.*

For Finding the Perfect Home

During times of transition, when people change residences, Jude is often asked to assist a client in finding the perfect home. She creates custom spell bags for them—they offer a list of specific needs, so it's a definite challenge. But we're happy to report that her bags work ... well ... like a charm.

As you assemble this bag, visualize your home clearly and exactly as you want it. Imagine what you need. See the colors of your home, breathe in the scent of the rooms, touch the banister or doorknobs, hear the creak of the floorboards, taste the fresh vegetables from the garden or the first meal you will eat there. See yourself and your family in the home surrounded by your belongings, which are all perfectly placed. Visualize this again as you hold the gris gris bag and enjoy its fragrance.

Bag Color:
Green or brown

Plants:
Allspice, aloe, carnation, cinnamon, chamomile, marigold petals, patchouli, willow

Metals:
Copper wire

Candle Color:
Brown

Day of the Week:
Monday

Calendar:
Waxing moon

Special Instructions:
Embellish this bag with a willow talisman; bend a thin, fresh willow branch into a circle, twist it together, and allow it to dry. You can fasten the talisman to the bag with natural hemp thread or jute twine.

Chant (speak three times):

> *A bit of spice, a bit of seed*
> *A bit of flavor, a bit of scent*
> *To bring about a want and need*
> *On which the heart and head are bent*
> *A dwelling safe, secure, and fine*
> *Of sound timber, fastened by love*
> *In haste and ease will soon be mine*
> *A perfect fit, as hand to glove*
> *I ask for guidance to this place*
> *That lives in my mind's eye*
> *A perfect blend of charm and grace*
> *Is waiting for me nigh.*

SPELLS FOR SPIRITUALITY
. . . .

"Spirituality" is an all-encompassing term. Whether we are grappling with issues of spiritual peace, death, psychic powers, dreaming, or creativity, our spiritual sensibilities come into play. Spirituality is inherently different than religion (though some argue to the contrary), and addresses an intricate part of ourselves that is elusive and amorphous. Some people believe that the spirit exists in two places at once—here in our reality, and also beyond the veil. They believe that we communicate with spirits through an innately pure energy, which constantly crosses back and forth like an alternating current.

Whatever your particular belief may be, your spiritual self will find a way to make its presence known in your life. The gris gris bags described below can be assembled to address various aspects of spirituality. Use these spells wisely, with an open heart and open mind.

For Cleansing

Before creating gris gris bags, it's imperative that you cleanse all sacred spaces and altars to remove negativity and promote harmony and peace. If your home needs a good cleaning as well, spread out the good work to all corners of the house. Burning incense or herbs such as cedar, juniper, and sage will consecrate your home, as will using a broom, preferably one made from birch, to ceremoniously brush away the negativity.

Bag Color:
Blue or white

Plants:
Anise, bay laurel, chamomile, chicory, cedar, cinquefoil, cloves, fennel, feverfew, hyssop, juniper, lemon, pine, rue, sage, thyme, vervain

Stones and Metals:
Amber, aquamarine, calcite, gold, jet, salt, selenite

Other Items:
Alligator teeth, soap, straw from a broom

Candle Color:
Blue or white

Day of the Week:
Saturday

Calendar:
Waning moon

Special Instructions:
If you wish to use stones in this gris gris bag, make sure they are recharged. You can do this by burning sage over them or placing them in salt water. Many people place stones under the full or new moon to gather alternate energies. Some stones need special cleansing techniques, so it's helpful to consult a magical stone manual first.

Chant:

> *I ask that all blessings enter this bag*
> *And that the power of the ingredients*
> *Bless and cleanse my home,*
> *My sacred space, my body.*

For Contacting Spirits

When it comes to spirits, there are a few things to remember before you begin making your bag. Always ask yourself what your true purpose is for contacting or connecting with the other side. Then approach the process as if you're visiting a friend. Open your heart to what your friend has to say, but remember that spirits speak to us in a unique way—they make unusual sounds, cause objects to fall, or even leave "hints" throughout the house like items out of place or open books. Keep an eye out for serendipitous connections to your past or meaningful images and numbers. Spirits send messages, sometimes issue warnings, and often they try to guide us.

The trick is to not fear these things as you interpret a spirit's intention. Of course, it is true that there are malevolent energies out there. We've found that using lilac incense or fresh-cut lilac blooms quells most types of negative spiritual energy.

When making your gris gris bag, have a photo handy of the person with whom you wish to make contact. Speak their name aloud or write it on paper, fold it up tight, and include it in the bag. If you're hoping to contact nonspecific ghosts or entities in your home, you may want to ask for their blessing while creating the bag, then appeal to them to visit in peace, love, and harmony. Lavender is especially good for making contact with spirits.

Be prepared to receive unexpected guests as you make this bag.

Bag Color:
Indigo or violet

Plants:
Black hellebore, four-leaf clover, dandelion, lavender, thyme

Stones:
Lapis lazuli, meteorite, moss agate, obsidian

Other Items:
Smoke, from incense or from burning an herb like sage or cedar, purifies the space and enhances communication with the spirits; this is good to have present when assembling the bag.

Candle:
Indigo, violet, white

Day of the Week:
Saturday

Calendar:
Waxing or full moon

Special Instructions:

It's important to keep the air as still as possible while working with spirits. Shut off all fans, heaters, air conditioners, and any other source of a breeze. If it's oppressively hot when you're doing your work, you can open a window, but the stiller the air, the more receptive and undisturbed the energy flow.

Chant:

> *I call to thee*
> *Through dark of night*
> *Who've walked the path*
> *And seek the light*
> *I listen well*
> *Tales unfold*
> *To words profound*
> *And secrets told.*

For Creativity

Writers and other artistic types love to connect with the Greek Muses, daughters of Zeus who represent the arts. Although the term "muse" has been woefully modulated (some would say bastardized) over the years, it is still synonymous with the idea of brilliant inspiration. The essence of the Muses, and the faith so many placed in them, lingers even today. Invoke the Muses while assembling your bag; in addition to the Greek Muses, you could call on Ireland's Brigit—the goddess of poetry, music, and the creative arts—to add her blessings to your creative endeavor.

Hazelnuts, also known as filberts, are said to provide great inspiration and creativity as well. You may either include them in your gris gris bag or enjoy some coated in chocolate while you work. (Chocolate always provides great inspiration, while the hazelnut is "lagniappe"—which means "a little something extra" in Louisiana lingo.)

Bag Color:
Orange or yellow

Plants:
Hazel, rue

Stones:
Aquamarine, citrine, fire agate, garnet, green tourmaline, malachite, red aventurine, sodalite, vanadinite

Other Items:
Anything that represents the nature of your creativity. For instance, writers may wish to include a book token while musicians may wish to include tokens of their instruments. Jude has a small collection of old fountain pens—adding one to the bag's exterior makes an effective talisman.

Candle Color:
Orange or yellow

Day of the Week:
Monday

Calendar:
Full moon, or waxing if you're developing new creative projects.

Special Instructions:
Write down your specific goals and desires, or the outline of your creative project, on a piece of paper and include it within your bag. If you're a poet, you may choose to write your intention in verse for a little added effect. Just make sure all the items, including the paper, add up to an odd number.

For Death & Rebirth

The herbs basil and rosemary were once commonly used at burials, possibly to bring about a more pleasant scent. Historically, rosemary was burned with juniper berries to disinfect hospitals. It was known for spiritual cleansing, to bring sweet dreams, as an herb of youth, and for remembrance.

The ancient Greeks placed thyme in coffins to ensure the soul's passage to the afterlife, and the Egyptians used the oil of thyme, a natural antiseptic, as an embalming fluid. Shakespeare called marigolds the funeral flower, while the Hindus see this yellow-gold plant as a symbol of life and eternity. To represent how life is everlasting, the evergreen cedar and the long-living yew are planted in graveyards and cemeteries. Yew has also been used in ceremonies to raise the dead, but we don't recommend going that far.

Bag Color:
Black or green

Plants:
Basil, cedar, elder, lotus, marigold, parsley, rosemary, thyme, yew

Stones:
Jade (for renewal)

Candle Color:
Black, green, or white

Day of the Week:
Saturday

Calendar:
New moon or blue moon

Chant:
The last lines of Edmund Spenser's Sonnet 75 make for a lovely recitation:

> *My verse your virtues rare shall eternize,*
> *And in the heavens write your glorious name.*
> *Where whenas death shall all the world subdue,*
> *Our love shall live, and later life renew.*

For Peace

We desire peace in all areas of our lives—the home, the workplace, the world at large. Peace can also be sought within ourselves through calming soul and mind, rephrasing thoughts and actions, and drawing closer to nature and the divine. Overall, peace begins with our spiritual sensibilities and spreads onward and outward from there. Use the following spell bag to work toward peace in everything you do ... for peace begins with each of us.

Bag Color:
Blue or white

Plants:
Basil, dandelion, lavender, marigold, myrtle, olive, passionflower, pennyroyal, vervain, witch hazel

Stones and Shells:
Azurite, blue aventurine, carnelian, coral, obsidian, onyx, quartz (clear), rose quartz, silver, tourmaline, white opal

Other Items:
Dove amulet or token (preferably a dove carrying an olive branch)

Candle:
White

Day of the Week:
Sunday

Calendar:
Waxing moon

Chant:

> *Peace be with me.*
> *Peace be with us all.*

For Psychic Powers

There are a multitude of exercises available to help enhance your psychic powers, and hundreds of workshops designed to train your spiritual energies and improve your intuitive abilities. All of these activities, however, are rooted in two fundamental states: focus and relaxation. Keep these two factors in mind when constructing your gris gris bag, which will stimulate your psychic powers and start you on your journey into intuition. Just allow your spiritual energies to surface, and trust your instincts as the messages start flowing. (For this spell, we recommend requesting divine assistance.)

Bag Color:
Silver or violet

Plants:
Bergamot, cinnamon, (four-leaf) clover, eucalyptus, lotus, mugwort, primrose, saffron, thyme

Stones:
Blue aventurine, amazonite, amethyst, azurite, celestite, citrine, emerald, lapis lazuli, opal, petrified wood (to connect with past lives), purple jade, selenite, turquoise

Other Items:
An ankh, scarab, other amulets

Candle Color:
Violet, silver, or white

Day of the Week:
Saturday

Calendar:
Waxing or full moon

Special Instructions:
Jude's method for achieving a psychic connection is to imagine a series of doors opening. The doors can look any way you like—elaborate,

or simple wood. Let your imagination flow. When each door opens, a new secret is revealed. The doors open faster and faster, and each one takes you on a journey farther away. This can prove to be an effective visual while you are moving into a meditative state.

For Sweet Dreams

Rather than creating the usual kind of gris gris bag for this spell, we suggest making a dream pillow. These are easily constructed—simply sew three sides of two equal pieces of fabric together, fill the pillowcase with the gris gris items, then sew the final side up. Or you can choose a piece of rectangular fabric, fold it in half, fill it up with items, and sew the three remaining sides together. Handkerchiefs or old doilies can also make great dream pillows, especially if they have some history behind them.

Once the pillow is finished, place it either on the side of your regular pillow, if there is no risk of it being disturbed, or beneath your pillow. (Because the dream pillow contains herbs and possibly powders and small stones, we wouldn't want anyone to accidentally ingest or inhale the ingredients should it break open in the night.) Not only does the dream pillow guarantee the sweetest of dreams, but the smell of the aromatic herbs alone will send you off to dreamland.

Bag Color:
Indigo

Plants:
Betony, chamomile, cinquefoil, crab apple, holly, jasmine, lavender, linden, mandrake, mimosa, marigold, mistletoe, passionflower, thyme, valerian, vervain

Stones and Shells:
Azurite, carnelian, citrine, coral, green jasper, hematite, jet, rose quartz, ruby, silver

Candle Color:
Indigo or white

Day of the Week:
Monday

Calendar:
Waxing or full moon

Special Instructions:
We recommend keeping a notepad and pen next to your bed so that when you awake, you can write down your dream experiences. Don't be fooled into thinking you will remember it later—dreams evaporate like water. Not only do you have better dream recall upon waking, but you will remember the feelings and colors of your dream as well, which are aspects that are important to note. Pay attention to the details of your dreams, even things that appear to have little meaning. The meaning may come to light as your day wears on.

For Prophetic Dreams

As with the Spell for Sweet Dreams, above, we encourage you to make a dream pillow instead of a standard gris gris bag, and place it near your pillow. This spell differs from the Spell for Sweet Dreams, however, in that it offers more than a good night's sleep devoid of nightmares. It will help bring about prophetic dreams, invoke answers to questions, and offer a glimpse into your future.

While creating this pillow (or bag, if you prefer), think carefully about your specific questions, problems, or concerns. Consider a particular project or situation in detail. After placing the bag by your pillow, you should receive your answers through your dreams. But always remember that the prophetic dream is only as effective as the memory of the dreamer.

Bag Color:
Silver or violet

Plants:
Ash, chamomile, cinquefoil, ivy, mugwort

Stones:
Azurite, moonstone (in India, prophetic dreams visit those who wear moonstone), selenite

Candle Color:
Violet, silver, or white

Day of the Week:
Monday

Calendar:
Waxing or full moon

Special Instructions:
As in the Spell for Sweet Dreams, we strongly recommend keeping a notepad and pen next to your bed so that you can write down your dream experiences. Remember to think about all aspects of your dreams and pay close attention to details.

Chant:

> As I sleep, I ask for all answers to all questions,
> For insight into my situation, light into my
> darkness.
> Upon waking, I will know what I need to do.

For Wisdom

Many herbs, plants, and stones have long associations with wisdom. Sage, for instance, represented wisdom to the Greeks, which is why we call wise men and women "sages." Hazelnuts were credited with giving the mythological Fintan wisdom after he swam (as a salmon) beneath a grove of hazel trees and ate the nuts. And no one can doubt the wisdom of the mighty oak tree that grows strong and lives a long life, or of the garnet, known in Buddhist and Hindu traditions for bringing wisdom to the owner. In the gris gris bag you make, you will be drawing on wisdom that is inherent in our Earth's creations. Soon you will recognize the brilliance that lies within us all.

Bag Color:
Purple or yellow

Plants:
Cinquefoil, hazel, oak, sage

Stones:
Garnet, lapis lazuli, meteorite

Other Items:
Owl and wizard charms or tokens

Candle:
Purple, yellow

Day of the Week:
Wednesday

Calendar:
Waxing or full moon

Special Instructions:
Place around yourself items representing people whose minds you admire, such as texts by Albert Einstein or William Shakespeare. Depending on the type of knowledge you wish to garner, think of figures throughout history who have served us in that particular area. If you're struggling with mathematics, place a compass or protractor nearby, and if it's geography that challenges you, use a stack of maps. Use your imagination to connect with the specific energy.

SPELLS FOR SELF-IMPROVEMENT
. . . .

Even the most beautiful people in the world have self-esteem issues. Everyone would like to improve their appearance, intelligence, or state of mind, and occasionally wants to start over, completely fresh. We'd love to shed bad habits like smoking and rid ourselves of troublesome behaviors like procrastination. Given our oh-so-human nature, there's always room for improvement.

The following gris gris spells are designed to help you achieve those little upgrades that will make life a bit easier. Whatever your weakness, there's nothing a little gris gris magic can't help you with. Remember, as always, that intention is everything. Sometimes the magic comes more from within us than from within the bag—it becomes a joint effort of the self as the combined powers work wonders. The key to any of these spells is to truly believe in your power to change.

For Beauty (internal and external)
There are several herbs and stones that represent external beauty in a gris gris bag. Avocado pits, for instance, are supposed to grant beauty to those who carry them. Maidenhair fern, soaked in water and allowed to dry, is said to induce beauty magic. Gold and amazonite, while not beauty-related stones per se, promote self-confidence, which may bring assurance to those who feel less than perfect.

When making this beauty bag, however, it is vital to remember that beauty is in the eye of the beholder. What we find beautiful may not seem so to others. This is why you must consider the inner aspects of beauty—such as that which comes from confidence, compassion, or a kind heart—as you build your gris gris. Keep in mind that the only eye that matters when it comes to your beauty is your own. Never try to become what others want you to be, or you will lose yourself in the battle.

Bag Color:
Pink

Plants:
Avocado pit, catnip, flax, ginseng, lotus, maidenhair fern, yerba santa

Stones, Metals, and Shells:
Amazonite, amber, cat's eye, copper, gold, opal, red jasper, scallop shells

Other Items:
Swan tokens

Candle Color:
Pink

Day of the Week:
Friday

Calendar:
Use a waning moon if you wish to eliminate something about yourself, such as excess weight. Use a waxing moon if your intention involves personal growth.

Chant:

> *I am beautiful. I am perfect.*
> *I am one with nature,*
> *And everything in nature is beautiful and perfect.*
> *The discerning eye*
> *Is clouded by my kind heart.*
> *And all of nature's beauty*
> *Lives now within me.*

For Eliminating Bad Habits

See *For Good Riddance* in the **Spells for Healing** section.

For Happiness

If you feel blue, take a walk in a garden, park, or woods. There's nothing like nature to restore equilibrium and bring happiness. And given the many sources of happiness in our lives, it is a wonder how quickly it can escape us. Yet happiness is often hard to embrace; it seems so amorphous, so hard to define. What is actually happening, however, is that we are failing to recognize it. At root, happiness is related to gratitude—it comes from noticing the good things in your life more than the bad things. While the gris gris bag described below will not create happiness for you per se, it can help you to open your eyes to your blessings and embrace them more fully.

We recommend gathering fresh herbs and stones during your excursions into nature. When put into your bag, these items will remind you of your sojourn outdoors and your feelings while there. If the herbs we suggest are hard to find, just pick some up at your local grocery, farmer's market, or nursery, and plant them in your garden or on a windowsill. A little greenery goes a long way toward building happiness (and you'll get fresh herbs for cooking as well as for your gris gris bag).

Bag Color:
White or yellow

Plants:
Basil, catnip, hawthorn, High John the Conqueror root, lavender, marjoram, mint, saffron, St. John's wort, vervain

Stones:
Agate

Candle Color:
White or yellow

Day of the Week:
Sunday

Calendar:
Waxing or full moon

Chant:

> *Though happiness at times eludes*
> *When sadness finally concludes*
> *I build my house on sacred shores*
> *Gratitude awaits at my doors*
> *A smile shall live upon my face*
> *My heart will fill with joy and grace*
> *Let blessed peace warm each room*
> *And cast away all thoughts of gloom.*

For Improving Memory

Former First Lady Eleanor Roosevelt used to take garlic tablets to improve her memory. It's hard to imagine why this brilliant woman felt the need for that type of assistance, but the garlic may have been what aided her in her myriad accomplishments. The early Arabs used rosemary to restore lost memory, and the ancient Greeks massaged rosemary oil into their foreheads to improve memory. The Romans believed sage could restore memory, and both rosemary and sage were used in burial ceremonies to remember those who had passed.

As vital as it is, memory is often taken for granted—until it is lost. Create your memory-improvement gris gris bag in honor and appreciation of this vital aspect of our lives.

Bag Color:
Black

Plants:
Garlic, rosemary, sage

Stones:
Emerald, garnet, rose quartz

Candle Color:
Black

Day of the Week:
Saturday

Calendar:
Waxing moon

Chant:

> *Of rosemary and sage,*
> *Restore my memory,*
> *Reveal all to me.*
> *Revive my yesterdays,*
> *Awaken my loves,*
> *Rebuild my world.*

For Joy

Herbs are truly one of the most joyous gifts the universe can offer. Chervil, a parsley-like herb, has been said to derive its botanical name, *cerefolium*, from the Latin for "leaves of joy." Chervil was known to cleanse the blood and also served as a bath additive and digestive aid (which are sources of joy in most people's lives!). Marjoram, derived from a term meaning "joy of the mountain," is known for its rich, aromatic leaves. Meanwhile, legend has it that simply gazing upon lavender brings joy to all. Saffron is believed to relieve melancholy; eating foods containing saffron will make you want to rejoice.

Creating a gris gris bag to bring about joy can be very rewarding. It's impossible not to smile as you gather these wonderful gifts from nature and mix them together by hand or grind them in your mortar and pestle. Crushing the leaves can trigger an aromatic euphoria as you imagine the extended joy resulting from your efforts. Enjoy!

Bag Color:
Orange

Plants:
Chervil, lavender, marjoram, olive, orange, saffron

Stones:
Hematite, ruby, turquoise

Candle Color:
Orange or white

Day of the Week:
Sunday

Calendar:
Waxing or full moon

Special Instructions:
Since all of the herbs used in this bag are edible, feel free to rub them freely into your palms and then run your fingers through your hair. The herbs' sweet and pungent oils will linger and bring with them a peaceful night's sleep.

For Maintaining Youth

The magic of youth cannot be overstated. It is the only time in our lives when we feel utterly infallible. We have the most energy, the strongest bodies, the sharpest (though often emptiest) minds, and a lust for life that will never be the same. Youth is the tempting elixir we barely get to taste before it is plucked from our hands. And while we cannot fight against the forward thrust of time, we live with the hope of being able to slow its progress.

This youth gris gris bag does not necessarily help you resist time's passage, but rather reminds you to celebrate that sweet elixir once again, regardless of your age. It tells us that we can be youthful, energetic, and excited about life's possibilities, joyful at the dawn of each new day of our lives. Be young again at heart; your true age is whatever age you feel.

Bag Color:
Pink

Plants:
Cat's eye, chervil, myrtle, palm, vervain

Stones:
Moonstone

Candle Color:
Pink

Day of the Week:
Saturday

Calendar:
Waxing or full moon

Chant:
Hold the gris gris bag in your dominant hand and recite the following chant:

> *Let me hold youth's promise within my palm,*
> *Never ignoring the conquering passage of time.*
> *May I face the years with a newfound calm,*
> *And embrace both youth and life sublime.*

For New Beginnings

Parsley makes a great addition to this gris gris bag. The ancient Greeks planted parsley at the edge of herb beds, which birthed the expression "being at the parsley and rue"—meaning to be at the beginning of an enterprise. Another good ingredient for your bag is birch bark. Soft and pliable, birch is the symbol for the first moon of the Celtic calendar, and therefore associated with new beginnings (see page 103). You may even choose to write your wish for a new beginning on the birch bark that you include in your bag.

Bag Color:
Green

Plants:
Birch, parsley

Stones and Shells:
Bloodstone, fire citrine, sand dollar, white zircon

Candle Color:
Green

Day of the Week:
Thursday

Calendar:
Waxing or full moon

Chant:

> *I stand at the threshold,*
> *Embarking on a new beginning*
> *And ask for blessings through this bag.*
> *Success will be mine.*
> *I will make it so.*

For Overcoming Difficulties
See the **Spells for Healing** section.

For Repelling Negativity
See the **Spells for Strength & Protection** section.

For Stopping Gossip
Gossip is a destructive force. It can do more damage than most people realize, destroying reputations, relationships, and even marriages.

It is difficult to defend yourself against those with a penchant for gossip, since a good story is often fairly enticing. But gossip is rarely accurate, and it's always hurtful. We can promise ourselves that we'll never participate in gossip, and this gris gris bag will help protect you from anyone who feels the need to gossip about you.

The trick with this spell bag is the idea of representation. A feather from a noisy bird, such as the mockingbird, and a photo of a talkative person are both perfect symbols for gossipmongers who need to be stopped. (You can use a photo of the offending gossiper, but it's not necessary.) Another option is to write "gossip" on a piece of paper, burn it, and place the ashes inside the bag. By doing this you are symbolically eliminating the desire to gossip from your environment, rather than just stopping one offender.

Bag Color:
Black

Plants:
Bay laurel, cloves, ginger, High John the Conqueror root, mint, nettles

Metals:
Copper

Other Items:
Feather of a noisy bird, a padlock (to shut a person up), an image of a face with the mouth crossed out

Candle:
Black

Day of the Week:
Saturday

Calendar:
Waning moon

Chant:

> *Halt the slander against my will,*
> *Let gossiping tongues be still*
> *Protect my spirit, mind, and place*
> *From vicious hearts and verbal waste.*

For Weight Loss

Cayenne pepper, a member of the chili family, does more than give food a nice, flavorful bite. In addition to improving circulation, cayenne has been shown to raise the body's metabolism and can cause some weight loss. But for this gris gris bag, the pepper goes in the bag and not in the stomach!

As with all of our spells that address health issues, a large part of the success of the bag depends on your own actions. Just putting cayenne in a gris gris and refusing to make the necessary lifestyle changes won't get you very far. You have to make the physical effort. After you take the initiative (i.e., after you make the bag), commit to a specific goal and work toward it every day. The bag will serve as constant reminder of your commitment to a healthier, thinner you. It will also serve as a spiritual aid as you move toward your goal.

Bag Color:
Pink

Plants:
Cayenne

Stones and Metals:
Copper, gold (for willpower), moonstone

Other Items:
Tape measure

Candle Color:
Pink

Day of the Week:
Friday

Calendar:
Waning moon

Special Instructions:
When you wake up in the morning, spend a few moments with your weight loss gris gris bag. Hold it in your hand and restate your commitment to live a healthier life. When you feel the urge to fall back into your old ways, hold the bag tightly in your left hand and remind your heart how important this goal is to you. Let the bag speak to you and offer you strength and resolve.

SPELLS FOR STRENGTH & PROTECTION

· · · · · · · · · · · · · · · ·

For thousands of years, people have used magical elements to infuse themselves with courage. They called upon the spirits of their ancestors to guide them and protect them when going into battle, or carried talismans (such as bear claws or the teeth of wildcats) to instill themselves with the ferocity of the creature. Feats of courage and strength fill the Bible, from David and Goliath to Samson and Delilah. Whether it's magical muscles or sheer fearlessness that leads to the lion's den, history is replete with examples of men and woman standing up against insurmountable odds.

Gris gris bags for strength, protection, repelling negativity.

Today's battles are far less daunting than the ones ancient peoples faced. With the exceptions of war and any time survival is on the line, most of us only have to call upon our inner strength when we face bosses, angry clients, the dentist, or our in-laws. But courage is courage, and sometimes it can be difficult to muster. The following gris gris bags will help you stir the sleeping strength and protective energy that lives within you. For ages, these ingredients have infused users with that extra edge when dealing with overwhelming situations.

For Courage

Before the Battle of Marathon, the Greeks chewed fennel to give themselves courage when fighting the Persians. Since fennel is believed to offer protection, it also enhances courage. Thyme can act as a stimulant when chewed, infusing warriors with audacity and confidence; Greek warriors used it, Roman soldiers bathed with thyme before battle, and English women of the Middle Ages gave knights tokens of thyme before sending them off to war. Thyme is also well-known for its medicinal properties in fighting off colds and flu, and was believed to guard against the plague. Through the ages, it has served to treat neurological disorders, including depression and anxiety.

Bag Color:
Red

Plants:
Black cohosh, fennel, thyme, yarrow

Stones, Metals, and Shells:
Bloodstone, carnelian, gold, onyx, red jade, ruby, pyrite, sand dollar, tiger's eye, tourmaline

Candle Color:
Red or orange

Day of the Week:
Tuesday

Calendar:
Waxing or full moon

Special Instructions:

Carry your bag to remind yourself of the courage that slumbers within you. If you are faced with a difficult situation, keep the bag on hand and enjoy the aroma before confronting your lions.

For Endurance

Ancient Egyptians carried fiery orange carnelian stones to renew their energy. In Indian mythology, the garnet was called "Kundalini fire," referencing the coiled energy that lies at the libidinal base of the spine (the sacral chakra); the rich redness of the garnet speaks directly to our sexuality, our creative spirit, and our stamina. The combined energies of these stones can instill both vitality and endurance. In a gris gris bag with the herbs listed below, they can help you keep on your path, maintain focus, and commit to completion of the task at hand.

Bag Color:
Orange

Plants:
Camellia, garlic, oak

Stones and Shells:
Bloodstone, carnelian, garnet, jasper, meteorite, mussel shells

Candle Color:
Orange

Day of the Week:
Tuesday

Calendar:
Waxing moon

For Protection

There are dozens of highly effective herbs you can use for protection, so choose those that speak directly to you. As always, the ingredients that call to you are often the best ones to include in your bag.

Protection amulets have a long, multicultural history—from holey stones (stones with natural holes) placed at the front door to turquoise worn to guard against evil—and can likewise be powerful ingredients in your gris gris bag. The Roman naturalist Pliny the Elder described amulets as having three basic categories of use: treating illness (medicinal), preventing illness, and protecting against misfortune.

Other items you might consider including in your protection bag are religious symbols that hold a special meaning for you. The ancient Egyptians enlisted the Eye of Horus to protect themselves against evil. You can use anything from saint medals to the Star of David; if the object connects with a special energy in your heart, by all means include it.

Bag Color:
Violet or white

Plants:
Aconite, angelica root, anise, ash, basil, bay laurel, birch, blackberry, black cohosh, bloodroot, buckeye, cinnamon, cinquefoil, three-leaf and four-leaf clover, cloves, cypress, devil's shoestring, dill, elder, eucalyptus, fennel, fern, fig, garlic, hazel, High John the Conqueror root, holly, hyssop, ivy, Job's tears, juniper, lemon verbena, lily, linden, lucky hand root, mandrake, marjoram, mimosa, mistletoe, mugwort, nettle, oak, oregano, palmetto, palm, pennyroyal, primrose, roses, rowan, sage, sunflower, valerian, vervain, willow, witch hazel, yarrow

Stones, Metals, and Shells:
Black jade, black tourmaline, coral, hematite, jet, ruby, sand dollar, serpentine, silver, tiger's eye, yellow and purple cowrie shells

Candle Color:
Blue or white

Day of the Week:
Saturday

Calendar:
Waxing or full moon

Chant:

> *By dark of night*
> *Or light of day*
> *Through clouded sky*
> *Or perfect sun*
> *Shield my spirit, body, mind*
> *From blessed hour*
> *Til day is done*
> *Follow me*
> *Through my Earthly charge*
> *Ease my path*
> *With every step*
> *Make my lessons*
> *Hard but kind*
> *And help to dry*
> *Each tear I've wept.*

For Repelling Negativity

Some would consider this gris gris bag a banishing spell (a spell used to ward off evil), but we prefer a less intimidating name, one that evokes positivity. Repelling negative aspects from our lives does not usually involve evil—it more often involves ridding ourselves of bad habits or self-deprecating thoughts, stopping ourselves from talking badly about a person, or simply cleansing a room of bad energy left over from an argument. Of course, this spell is effective in banishing evil as well, but in the case of people doing you harm, you may want to consider implementing the Spell for Good Riddance (see page 183).

Bag Color:
Black

Plants:
Basil, betony, black hellebore, caraway seeds, cedar, chamomile, chervil, clover, cloves, cypress, crab apple, devil's shoestring, elder, fennel, fern, feverfew, ginseng, holly, hyssop, juniper, lily, mandrake, marjoram, mistletoe, mugwort, nettle, oak, pennyroyal, pine, plantain, rosemary, rowan, rue, sage, sainfoin, St. John's wort, thyme, watercress, yarrow

Stones and Metals:
Amethyst, aquamarine, black onyx, black tourmaline, bloodstone, copper (when combined with mimosa seeds), garnet, hematite, jet, malachite, obsidian, smoky quartz

Candle Color:
Black, white, or violet

Day of the Week:
Saturday

Calendar:
Waning moon

Chant:

> *I call forth spirits and the power of the herbs and stones to cleanse this space,*
> *This home, my person, and to drive all negativity away.*
> *I ask for blessings in its wake and protection from all further negativity.*

For Strength

Think about strength. What constitutes strength? What embodies strength? Heracles, the Greek hero and demigod of mythic physique, power, and cunning, might come to mind. The Assyrians and Babylonians honored the bull as an image of strength. Images of historically brawny figures or powerful animals make good additions to this gris gris bag.

Because of their hardness, stones are also good candidates for the bag. Iron and diamonds are famous for their hardness and potency. Hematite is interesting here as well; it is usually black, gray, or red, and the red variety can be ground to rich, red powder that is often used as a pigment. The name "hematite" comes from the Greek word for "blood red stone"; the Greeks saw the value of the life's blood within this intensely hard stone. Also, because of its magnetic properties (though not all hematite is magnetized), it is associated with containing energy and having the ability to draw in other energies.

Regarding herbs, bay leaves relate to prowess in sports, and garlic was thought to repel vampires. Overall, consider the attributes and historical uses of the items you wish to include in your strength spell bag.

Bag Color:
Orange

Plants:
Bay laurel, betony, garlic, mugwort, pennyroyal, saffron, St. John's wort

Stones, Metals, and Shells:
Beryl, bloodstone, diamond, hematite, iron, iron nails, jasper, mussel shells, onyx, tiger's eye, red tourmaline

Other Items:
Images such as Hercules, Atlas shouldering the world, or Scotland's Muilidheartach; images of oxen, bulls, bears, tigers, even mules, depending on your purpose.

Candle Color:
Orange

Day of the Week:
Tuesday

Calendar:
Waxing or full moon

Chant:

> *I ask these herbs, stones, and talismans to give me strength.*
> *Our shared nature flows through my veins.*

For Warding Off Bad Dreams

See also *For Sweet Dreams* in the **Spells for Spirituality** section.

The only difference between this gris gris bag and the bag described in the Spell for Sweet Dreams entry is that the herbs and stones listed below are specific for warding off nightmares. Thyme, for instance, has been recommended for curing nightmares, and also is an effective relief for anxiety (which can be the cause of bad dreams). But feel free to also use any of the ingredients listed in the Spell for Sweet Dreams, if you are so inclined, and you can create either a bag or a dream pillow (see the Spell for Sweet Dreams for instructions on sewing your dream pillow).

Bag Color:
Black

Plants:
Betony, thyme

Stones and Shells:
Amethyst, coral

Candle Color:
Black, white, or violet

Day of the Week:
Saturday

Calendar:
Waning moon

Chant:

>*Darkness no more*
>*Will cross my door*
>*Divine light beams*
>*Restores my dreams.*

SPELLS FOR SAFE TRAVEL & WEATHER

· · · · · · · · · · · · · · · · ·

We travel a lot in our work, so naturally we carry safe-travel gris gris bags with us and wear emeralds and moonstone for safe passage. Many of our friends carry items from home, such as photos, small toys from their kids, and pocket tokens such as rabbit's feet, lucky coins, or stones to touch at any moment. Cheré carries a small toy Pegasus that was owned by her son when he was young. She found it in her luggage years ago and it's remained there ever since, a guardian angel while traveling. Jude prefers lucky stones found on the beach, the ones with unhindered circular lines running through them, which signify a smooth journey. They remind her of Aunt Alyce, who surely watches over her, and whose trips to the beach on Cape Cod always meant a bounty of shells and stones.

Gris gris bags for safe travel and protection against storms.

Travelers have been carrying lucky items for centuries. In the United States, pioneers who reached Ohio discovered the round nut of the buckeye tree, which is perfect for carrying in your pocket and rubbing like a worry stone. They brought the buckeye back east and it became a lucky traveler's object. And you may recall the medallion of St. Christopher, the patron saint of travelers in the Catholic church, which often adorns car dashboards.

Even today, with all the advances in travel technology, embarking on a journey sparks worry. We are separated from our loved ones for days at a time, we brave the whims of weather, fate, and other travelers, and we feel removed from our lives, even if for a brief period. It is no wonder that we seek protection whether on the road, in the air, or on the ocean.

Below, we offer suggestions for specific safe travel gris gris bags, but in the end it all comes down to you. If you have an object, token, or personal stone that makes you feel safe, by all means use it. Let it work its magic on you as it can no other.

There are also several spells for the weather, and many of the herbs and stones listed for these bags have been associated with weather since the time of the ancients. Their protection powers and rain-making magic are legendary.

For Fishermen

Fishermen need all the luck they can get. Not only do they face the dangers of the deep, but they must find fish in the vast stretches of water that make up bayous, rivers, lakes, and oceans. Hawthorn leaves in a gris gris bag should do the trick, along with cinquefoil and an aquamarine. The herb cinquefoil, in fact, is the patron herb of fishermen and one that brings luck.

Bag Color:
Blue

Plants:
Anise oil, ash, cinquefoil, hawthorn

Stones and Shells:
Amethyst, aquamarine, coral

Other Items:
Fish tokens, an image of a pair of eyes (fishermen paint them on boats to ward off the evil eye), lures

Candle Color:
Blue

Day of the Week:
Wednesday

Calendar:
Waxing or full moon

Special Instructions:
St. Lucy, the patron saint of those who are blind, helps fishermen find the best spots. You may want to include an image of St. Lucy in your bag.

For Safe Travel

St. John the Baptist donned a girdle of mugwort before entering the wilderness—he knew about the power of natural elements to protect us. Stones such as beryl, malachite, and emerald have long been associated with safe travel. If you wish to invoke the assistance of ancient gods, Mercury is the god of travel.

Bag Color:
Blue

Plants:
Ash, comfrey, feverfew, mandrake, mugwort, oregano

Stones, Metals, and Shells:
Aluminum, beryl, coral, emerald, jacinth, jet, malachite, meteorite, moonstone, silver, turquoise

Candle Color:
Blue

Day of the Week:
Wednesday

Calendar:
Waxing or full moon

Chant:

> *Dead of night and dead of day*
> *Watch me on my Earthly way,*
> *Glow of moon and air of night*
> *Guide me through with gifted sight*
> *Open portals long since sealed*
> *Bathe in light 'til wounds are healed*
> *Fill me now with hope and gain*
> *As I shed my desirous bane*
> *Now I see my path is cleared*
> *Banished of all things once feared.*

For Sailors & Those Traveling by Ship

Sailors carried crosses made from ash trees for protection at sea, and ships were routinely constructed from cypress wood because of its resistance to rot. Both are examples of effective herbs to use in a safe passage by boat gris gris bag. For those of you with Catholic roots, carry, in a black bag, a blessed mandrake root with four Masses said over it.

Bag Color:
Blue

Plants:
Ash, rosemary, wormwood

Stones, Metals, and Shells:
Amethyst, aquamarine, beryl, coral, mottled jasper, pearls, petrified wood, silver

Other Items:
Dolphin or Poseidon amulets or tokens

Candle Color:
Blue

Day of the Week:
Wednesday

Calendar:
Waxing or full moon

For Soldiers

Most gris gris bags created for this spell are used for strength and courage in battle and protection from harm. Fennel and thyme gave courage to the Greeks and Romans. English knights received tokens of thyme before heading off to war. St John's wort is reported to make soldiers unbeatable. If you wish to avoid military service, add a four-leaf clover to the bag.

Bag Color:
Blue

Plants:
Ash, black cohosh, four-leaf clover (for avoiding military service), fennel, High John the Conqueror root, St. John's wort, thyme, yarrow

Stones and Shells:
Amethyst, hematite, red jade, ruby, pyrite, sand dollar, tiger's eye

Other Items:
Military tokens or medals

Candle Color:
Blue

Day of the Week:
Tuesday

Calendar:
Waxing or full moon

Special Instructions:
This could also be a good time to honor military ancestors by including an item they carried into battle.

For Weather: To Bring Rain

People always say that if you want it to rain, go wash your car. There's a lot of truth in that statement. Consider how much thought you give the weather when you wash your car—much more than usual. Thoughts control so much of our environment, but we only think about the weather when it causes a problem directly for us. This is why creating a bag of intention to bring rain will work—if you just believe.

Bag Color:
White, black, or indigo

Plants:
Heather, ferns, pansy, rice

Stones:
Agate, bloodstone, jasper

Other Items:
Cotton, frog tokens

Candle Color:
White, black, or indigo

Day of the Week:
Saturday

Calendar:
Waxing moon

Chant:

> *Ancients hear my plea,*
> *Return the rain to me,*
> *A thirsty Earth awaits,*
> *Parched soil do abate,*
> *We welcome storm and cloud,*
> *And rolling thunder loud,*
> *To drench the hill and plain,*
> *And thrive once again.*

For Weather: Protection Against Storms

Cheré loves the violent thunderstorms that roll through Louisiana, but her Boston terrier doesn't enjoy them one bit—Mocha crawls into her bed, shaking, until the storm passes. This fear is not uncommon among both people and animals. Jude has always held a healthy respect for the dangers of lightning, since one of her father's favorite tales of his youth was the time when a bolt came through the front door and deflected off a radiator to hit him in his behind. The scar was a constant reminder to him of the unwieldy and merciless power coming from the sky. Even the Roman emperor Tiberius wore a wreath of bay laurels on his head as he slept, to avoid being struck by lightning. There are, in fact, several wonderful herbs thought to possess power against lightning and storms; mistletoe does double duty by protecting against both.

If you'd like to implore assistance from a deity, the list is plentiful. The Greek god Zeus, the Hindu god Indra, and the Norse god Thor all represent thunder. Other thunder gods include Jupiter (Roman), Ukko (Finnish), Susanoo (Japanese), Set (Egyptian), and the Thunderbird of early Native American cultures, to name only a few. Discover which deity speaks most clearly to you and seek their guidance.

Bag Color:
White, black, or indigo

Plants:
Acorn, bay laurel, birch, cedar, elder, hazel, holly, mistletoe, St. John's wort, vervain

Stones:
Agate, beryl, bloodstone, carnelian, flint, jade

Candle Color:
White, black, or indigo

Day of the Week:
Saturday

Calendar:
Waxing moon

Special Instructions:
Carry the bag with you during storms, but don't be foolish. Take the usual precautions and never tempt fate.

Chant:

> *Oh god of thunder*
> *Guide me well*
> *We honor you*
> *With this spell*
> *Your power lives*
> *Beyond our scope*
> *Protect us as*
> *We need and hope*
> *Spare us all*
> *Your anger, wrath*
> *And guide us safely*
> *Down our path.*

Growing a
Gris Gris Garden

CULTIVATING YOUR OWN HERBS

· · · · · · · · · · · · · · · ·

One of the joys of creating gris gris bags and spell sachets is incorporating the natural ingredients that resonate with you. Some people adore the smell of lavender, for instance, and a bag of intention drifting this sweet aroma will remind the owner of what's coming every time she smells the relaxing scent. Aromatherapists insist the smell of eucalyptus uplifts the mind and offers clarity of thought, not to mention opening the sinuses and clearing the lungs of congestion. It works against both mental and physical fatigue, and is even said to increase the activity of your brain waves.

Growing your own herbs, particularly those that you feel a special affinity for, is empowering. When you add these ingredients to your spell sachet, the awareness that you have grown them, harvested them, and dried them yourself greatly increases the power and ownership of your intention.

In addition, growing your own herbs removes the threat of the over-harvesting of certain plants. And when you pick your own herbs for use in your bag, you have the opportunity to thank Mother Earth for her bounty and magical properties, something not possible with commercial herb production.

The lists below name herbs, flowers, and trees that can be grown in groups to create gardens with specific intentions. Most of the plants mentioned are fairly easy to obtain and grow, and most thrive in a variety of climates. Before you plant, however, check with gardening experts, a good herb or gardening book, or an online source to make sure your soil and climate are adequate. Find out what needs your plants may have, such as full sun or partial shade, moist soil or dry conditions. Another thing to consider is companion planting. Eucalyptus planted by citrus, for instance, helps ward off pests from the fruit.

Many of these herbs may be grown indoors as well, or in containers and pots placed on decks, patios, and small spaces outside. Some plants may help protect or attract good fortune when placed inside the house in specific spots. A potted bay laurel, for example, should be positioned by the front door for protection.

Anglo-Saxon Sacred Herb Garden

Chamomile, chervil, crab apple, fennel, mugwort, nettle, plantain, betony or sainfoin, watercress.

Culinary Herb Garden

Basil, dill, fennel, fenugreek, garlic, mint, oregano, parsley, rosemary, saffron, sage, thyme.

Good Fortune & Luck Herb Garden

Bay laurel, black-eyed peas, buckeye, ferns, hazel, High John the Conqueror root, holly, ivy, Job's tears, linden, lucky hand root, mojo beans, moss, oak, olive, orange, palm, parsley, pine, sunflower, yarrow. *For luck in gaming:* devil's shoestring, High John the Conqueror root, lucky hand root. *For luck in court:* cinquefoil.

Happiness Herb Garden

Basil, catnip, chamomile, jasmine, lavender, marjoram, mint, olive, saffron, vervain.

Healing Herb Garden

Apple, blackberry, cinquefoil, crab apple, cypress, eucalyptus, fennel, garlic, ginseng, hyssop, Job's tears, juniper, mandrake, marjoram, mimosa, mistletoe, mugwort, nettle, nutmeg, olive, pine, roses, rowan, rue, saffron, sage, St. John's wort, walnut, willow, witch hazel.

Hearth & Home Herb Garden

Apple, birch, caraway seeds, dandelion, pennyroyal. *For fertility:* apple, crab apple, fig, ginseng, hazel, mandrake, mistletoe, myrtle, nutmeg, oak, olive, palm, pine, rice, sunflower, walnut, willow. *For cats:* catnip, valerian. *For dogs:* anise.

Love Herb Garden

Anise, apple, basil, black cohosh, caraway seeds, catnip, cedar, cinnamon, cinquefoil, cloves, dandelion, fig, ginger, ginseng, ivy, jasmine, lavender, lemon verbena, linden, mandrake, marigold, marjoram, mistletoe, myrtle, nutmeg, olive, orange, pine, primrose, rosemary, roses, rowan, rue, saffron, St. John's wort, valerian, vervain, willow, yarrow. *For a good marriage:* apple, ivy, lavender, marjoram, orange, pine, rosemary. *For passion:* cayenne, cinnamon, dill, fenugreek, ginger, nettle, palm, palmetto, rosemary, roses, saffron.

Peace Herb Garden

Basil, dandelion, lavender, marigold, myrtle, olive, passionflower, pennyroyal, vervain, witch hazel.

Prosperity Herb Garden

Angelica root, ash, basil, bay laurel, birch, blackberry, black-eyed peas, camellia, cedar, chamomile, cinquefoil, clover, cloves, comfrey, dandelion, dill, echinacea, fenugreek, ferns, fig, ginger, High John the Conqueror root, lucky hand root, mandrake, mint, mojo beans, moss, myrtle, nutmeg, oak, orange, palm, pecan, pine, rice, sage, vervain.

Protection Herb Garden

Aconite, angelica root, anise, ash, basil, bay laurel, birch, blackberry, black cohosh, buckeye, cinnamon, cinquefoil, clover, cloves, cypress, devil's shoestring, dill elder, eucalyptus, fennel, fern, fig, garlic, hazel, High John the Conqueror root, holly, hyssop, ivy, Job's tears, juniper, lemon verbena, lily, linden, lucky hand root, mandrake, marjoram, mimosa, mistletoe, mugwort, nettle, oak, palmetto, palm, pennyroyal, primrose, roses, rowan, sage, sunflower, valerian, vervain, willow, witch hazel, yarrow. *For protection from accidents:* feverfew, mistletoe. *For protection while traveling:* ash, comfrey, mandrake, mugwort.

Purification Herb Garden

Anise, bay laurel, cedar, chamomile, chicory, cinquefoil, fennel, feverfew, hyssop, lavender, lemon verbena, lily, lotus, palm, pine, rosemary, rue, sage, thyme, valerian, vervain.

Spirituality Herb Garden

Bergamot, black hellebore, cinnamon, clover, dandelion, lotus, mugwort, primrose, saffron, thyme.

Strength, Endurance & Courage Herb Garden

Bay laurel, betony, black cohosh, camellia, fennel garlic, lemon verbena, oak, saffron, St. John's wort, thyme, walnut, willow, yarrow, yew.

Sweet & Prophetic Dreams Herb Garden

Ash, betony, chamomile, cinquefoil, crab apple, holly, lavender, linden, mandrake, mimosa, marigold, mistletoe, mugwort, passionflower, thyme, valerian, vervain.

Bibliography

Andrews, Ted. *Animal Speak: The Spiritual & Magical Powers of Creatures Great and Small.* Woodbury, MN: Llewellyn, 2002.

"American Indian Bags." http://www.native-languages.org/bags.htm (accessed January 2009).

Arkins, Diane C. *Halloween: Romantic Art and Customs of Yesteryear.* New Orleans: Pelican Publishing, 2000.

Atwood, Mary Dean. *Spirit Healing: How to Make Your Life Work.* New York: Sterling, 2006.

Bach, Marcus. *Strange Sects and Curious Cults.* New York: Dodd, Mead & Company, 1961.

Bahn, Paul. *Ancient World in Your Pocket.* New York: Barnes & Noble/Elwin Street Productions, 2007.

Baker, Margaret. *Gardener's Magic and Folklore.* New York: Universe Books, 1978.

Bibb, Henry. "On the Use of Roots and Powders Among the Slaves," 1849 (excerpt). http://www.southern-spirits.com/bibb-roots-powders-slaves.html (accessed February 2009).

Bierlein, J. F. *Living Myths: How Myth Gives Meaning to Human Experience.* New York: Ballantine/Wellspring, 1999.

Binder, Pearl. *Magic Symbols of the World.* London: The Hamlyn Publishing Group, 1972.

Bird, Stephanie Rose. *Sticks, Stones, Roots & Bones: Hoodoo Mojo & Conjuring Herbs.* Woodbury, MN: Llewellyn, 2004.

Blanchard, Richard, trans. *Witchcraft Grimore.* Palm Springs, CA: International Guild of Occult Sciences, 1993.

Blavatsky, H. P. "The Number Seven." http://www.blavatsky.net/blavatsky/arts/NumberSeven.htm (accessed August 2008).

Bodin, Ron. *Voodoo: Past and Present.* Lafayette, LA: The Center for Louisiana Studies, University of Louisiana at Lafayette, 1990.

Bonner, Campbell. *Studies in Magical Amulets.* Ann Arbor, MI: University of Michigan Press, 1950.

Botkin, B. A., ed. *A Treasury of Mississippi River Folklore.* New York: American Legacy Press, 1955.

———, ed. *A Treasury of Southern Folklore.* New York: American Legacy Press, 1977.

Bowes, Susan. *Notions and Potions, A Safe, Practical Guide to Creating Magic and Miracles.* New York: Sterling Publishing, 1997.

Bremness, Lesley. *The Complete Book of Herbs: A Practical Guide to Growing and Using Herbs.* New York: Viking Studio, 1988.

Buckland, Raymond. *Scottish Witchcraft & Magick: The Craft of the Picts.* Woodbury, MN: Llewellyn, 2005.

Budge, E. A. Wallis. *Amulets and Superstitions.* New York: Dover Publications, 1978.

Cajun, Andre. *Louisiana Voodoo*. New Orleans: Harmanson Publisher, 1946.

Campbell, Joseph. *The Power of Myth with Bill Moyers*. New York: Doubleday, 1988.

———. *The Power of Myth with Bill Moyers*. New York: Mystic Fire Video. A Production of Apostrophe S Production with Public Affairs Television, Inc and Alvin H. Perlmutter, Inc., 1990.

"Celestia Avery: Tales of Conjure and Luck, from 'Georgia Slave Narratives." Two interviews conducted by Minnie B. Ross for the Federal Writers Project of the Works Progress Administration, 1936, 1937. http://www.southern-spirits.com/avery-conjure.html (accessed February 2009).

"The Celtic Connection." http://Wicca.com (accessed January 2009).

Christoph, Henning, and Hans Oberlander. *Voodoo, Secret Power in Africa*. Cologne, Germany: Taschen, 1996.

"Color: Meaning, Symbolism and Psychology." http://www.squidoo.com/colorexpert (accessed August 2008).

"Conjure Craft: Hoodoo, Rootwork and Conjuring for the 21st Century." http://www.llewellynjournal.com/article/504 (accessed December 2008).

Crockett, James Underwood. *Trees*. New York: Time-Life Books, 1972.

Culpeper, Nicholas. *Culpeper's Complete Herbal*. Berkshire, U.K.: Foulsham, 1975.

Cunningham, Scott. *Cunningham's Encyclopedia of Magical Herbs*. Woodbury, MN: Llewellyn, 2000.

Densmore, Frances. *How Indians Use Wild Plants for Food, Medicine and Crafts*. New York: Dover Publications, 1974.

Dolnick, Barrie. *Simple Spells for Success, Ancient Practices for Creating Abundance and Prosperity*. New York: Harmony Books, 1996.

Dunwich, Gerina. *The Wicca Spellbook, A Witch's Collection of Wiccan Spells, Potions and Recipes*. New York: Citadel Press, 1994.

Dyer, Wayne. *There's a Spiritual Solution to Every Problem*. New York: Harper Collins, 2001.

Edwards, Tryon, C. N. Catrevas, Jonathan Edwards, and Ralph Emerson Browns. *The New Dictionary of Thoughts: A Cyclopedia of Quotations*. New York: StanBook, 1977.

Evans-Pritchard, E. E. *Witchcraft, Oracles and Magic Among the Azande*. New York: Oxford University Press, 1976.

Faulkner, Raymond O., trans. *Ancient Egyptian Book of the Dead*. New York: Barnes & Noble, 2005.

Fisher, Sally. *The Square Halo & Other Mysteries of Western Art Images and the Stories that Inspired Them*. New York: Harry N. Abrams, 1995.

Fontenot, Wonda L. *Secret Doctors: Ethnomedicine of African Americans*. Santa Barbara, CA: Bergin and Garvey, 1994.

Freeman, Mara. *Kindling the Celtic Spirit: Ancient Traditions to Illumine Your Life Through the Seasons*. New York: Harper Collins, 2001.

Gardner, Gerald Brousseau. "British Charms, Amulets and Talismans." *Folk-Lore* 53 (1942): 95–103.

Gaskell, G. A. *Dictionary of All Scriptures and Myths.* New York: Avenel Books, 1960.

Gibran, Kahlil. *The Prophet.* New York: Alfred A. Knopf, 1998.

Gonzalez-Wippler, Migene. *The Complete Book of Amulets & Talismans.* Woodbury, MN: Llewellyn, 2002.

Gregg, Susan. *The Complete Illustrated Encyclopedia of Magical Plants.* Beverly, MA: Fair Winds, 2008.

Grieve, Margaret. *A Modern Herbal.* New York: Dover Publications, 1971.

———. *A Modern Herbal.* http://botanical.com (accessed August 2008 to March 2009).

Grun, Bernard. *The Timetables of History: A Horizontal Linkage of People and Events.* New York: Touchstone Books, 1982.

Guiley, Ellen. *The Encyclopedia of Witches and Witchcraft.* New York: Facts On File, 2008.

Hall, Judy. *The Encyclopedia of Crystals.* Gloucester, MA: Fair Winds Press, 2006.

Hall, Manly P. *The Secret Teachings of All Ages.* New York: Jeremy P. Tarcher/Penguin, 2003.

Halliwell, James Orchard. *Popular Rhymes and Nursery Tales.* London: John Russell Smith, 1849.

Hart, Frederick. *Art: A History of Painting, Sculpture, Architecture.* New York: Prentice Hall and Harry N. Abrams, 1993.

Hearn, Lafcadio. "New Orleans Superstitions." Harper's Weekly 1886. http://www.southern-spirits.com/avery-conjure.html (accessed February 2009).

Heaven, Ross, and Howard G. Charing. *Plant Spirit Shamanism: Traditional Technique for Healing the Soul.* Rochester, VT: Destiny Books, 2006.

Hildburgh, Walter Leo. "Psychology Underlying the Employment of Amulets." *Folk-Lore* 62 (1952): 231–251.

Hill, Napoleon. *Think and Grow Rich.* Meriden, CT: The Ralston Society, 1937.

"The Holly and the Ivy Lore–Christmas Plants." http://www.anglian gardener.co.uk/Lore/christmas.htm (accessed January 2009).

Hopman, Ellen Evert. *A Druid's Herbal for the Sacred Earth Year.* Rochester, VT: Destiny Books, 1995.

Hylton, William H., and Clair Kowalchik, eds. *Rodale's Illustrated Encyclopedia of Herbs.* Emmaus, PA: Rodale, 1998.

Illes, Judika. *The Element Encyclopedia of Witch Craft: A Complete A-Z for the Entire Magical World.* London: Harper Element, 2005.

"Indian Bahai Temple." http://www.bahaindia.org (accessed March 2009).

"John the Conqueror." http://www.luckymojo.com/johntheconqueror.html (accessed January 2009).

K, Amber. *True Magick, A Beginner's Guide (second edition).* Woodbury, MN: Llewellyn, 2006.

Kane, Harnett T. *The Bayous of Louisiana.* New York: Bonanza Books, 1944.

Kaplan, Justin D., ed., and W. D. Ross, trans. *The Pocket Aristotle.* New York: Washington Square Press (Simon & Schuster), 1958.

Keville, Kathy. "Aromatherapy: Eucalyptus." http://health.howstuff-works.com/aromatherapy-eucalyptus.htm (accessed April 2009).

Kunz, George Frederick. *The Curious Lore of Precious Stones.* New York: Dover Publications, 1971.

Kynes, Sandra. *Whispers from the Woods, The Lore & Magic of Trees.* Woodbury, MN: Llewellyn, 2006.

———. *Your Altar: Creating a Sacred Space for Prayer and Meditation.* Woodbury, MN: Llewellyn, 2007.

Lalonde, Roxanne. "Unity in Diversity: Acceptance and Integration in an Era of Intolerance and Fragmentation." Master's thesis, Department of Geography, Carleton University Ottawa, Ontario, Canada, published April 1994. http://bahai-library.org/theses/unity.diversity.html (access date unknown).

Lavine, T. Z. *From Socrates to Sartre: The Philosophic Quest.* New York: Bantam Books, 1984.

Lawle, Julia. *The Illustrated Encyclopedia of Essential Oils: The Complete Guide to the Use of Oils in Aromatherapy and Herbalism.* New York: Barnes & Noble Books, 1995.

"The Lotus Symbol in Buddhism." http://www.religionfacts.com/buddhism/symbols/lotus.htm (accessed March 2009).

Malbrough, Ray T. *Charms, Spells, and Formulas.* Woodbury, MN: Llewellyn, 2002.

Malesky, Gale, and the editors of Prevention Health Books. *Nature's Medicines*. Emmaus, PA: Rodale, 1999.

McCoy, Edain. *Witta: An Irish Pagan Tradition*. St. Paul, MN: Llewellyn, 1998.

Measuring the Immeasurable: The Scientific Case for Spirituality (multiple contributors). Boulder, CO: Sounds True, 2008.

Medici, Marina. *Good Magic*. New York: Prentice Hall Press, 1988.

Meola, Kalyan V. "The Psychology of Color." *Hohonu, A Journal of Academic Writing*. University of Hawaii at Hilo Hawaii Community College. http://www.uhh.hawaii.edu/academics/hohonu/writing.php?id=73 (accessed August 2008).

Mercier, Patrica. *Chakras, Balance Your Body's Energy for Health and Harmony*. London: Godsfield Press, 2000.

Metzger, Bruce M., and Michael D. Coogan, eds. *The Oxford Companion to the Bible*. New York: Oxford University Press, 1993.

Miller, George A. "The Magical Number Seven, Plus or Minus Two: Some Limits on Our Capacity for Processing Information." *The Psychological Review* 63 (1956): 81–97.

"Mojo Hand and Root Bag." http://www.luckymojo.com/mojo.html (accessed January 2009).

Morrison, Dorothy. *Bud, Blossom and Leaf: The Magical Herb Gardener's Handbook*. Woodbury, MN: Llewellyn, 2001.

Moura, Ann. *Green Witchcraft, Folk Magic, Fairy Lore and Herb Craft*. Woodbury, MN: Llewellyn, 1999.

Murphy-Hiscock, Arin. *The Way of the Green Witch*. Cincinnati, OH: Provenance Press, 2006.

Oliver, Paul. *World Religions*. Chicago: Contemporary Books (McGraw-Hill), 2001.

Osbon, Diane K., ed. *A Joseph Campbell Companion: Reflections on the Art of Living*. New York: Harper Collins, 1991.

Paine, Sheila. *Amulets: Sacred Charms of Power and Protection*. Rochester, VT: Inner Traditions, 2004.

Peschek-Bohmer, Flora, and Gisela Schreiber. *Healing Crystals and Gemstones, From Amethyst to Zircon*. Old Saybrook, CT: Konecky & Konecky, 2003.

Picton, Margaret. *The Book of Magical Herbs: Herbal History, Mystery and Folklore*. Hauppauge, NY: Barrons, 2000.

Pinckney, Roger. *Blue Roots, African-American Folk Magic of the Gullah People*. Woodbury, MN: Llewellyn, 1998.

Puckett, Newbell Niles. *Folk Beliefs of the Southern Negro*. New York: Kensington, 2003.

Rasiwala, Eliza. "The Bahá'í House of Worship." http://www.baha india.org/temple/bahapur.html (accessed September 2010).

The Rodale Herb Book: How to Use, Grow, and Buy Nature's Miracle Plants. Emmaus, PA: Rodale, 1974.

Rolleston, T. W. *Celtic Myths and Legends*. New York: Dover Publications, Inc., 1990.

Ryan, Robert E., Ph.D. *The Strong Eye of Shamanism: A Journey Into the Caves of Consciousness*. Rochester, VT: Inner Traditions, 1999.

Saxon, Lyle, Edward Dreyer, and Robert Tallant. *Gumbo YaYa, Folk Tales of Louisiana* (Works Progress Association). New Orleans: Pelican Publishing, 1987.

Schanche, Don Jr. "Ancient Beliefs Still Alive in Georgia." *The Macon Telegraph*, circa 2000. http://www.southern-spirits.com/avery-conjure.html (accessed February 2009).

Schlosser, Katherine K., ed. *The Herb Society of America's Essential Guide to Growing and Cooking With Herbs*. Baton Rouge, LA: LSU Press, 2007.

"Seven Sacred Woods." www.sevensacredwoods.com (accessed December 2008).

Sheen, Joanna. *Potpourri: Creating Gifts with Long-Lasting Natural Fragrances*. London: Cassell, 1992.

"Skeleton of 12,000-Year-Old Shaman Discovered Buried with Leopard, 50 Tortoises and Human Foot." http://www.sciencedaily.com/releases/2008/11/081105083721.htm (accessed September 2010).

Simmons, Robert, and Naisha Ahsian. *The Book of Stones: Who They Are & What They Teach*: Berkeley, CA: North Atlantic Books, 2007.

Smith, Andrew F. *Oxford Encyclopedia of Food and Drink in America*. New York: Oxford University Press, 1976.

Spence, Lewis. *Ancient Egypt Myths and Legends*. Boston: David D. Nickerson & Co., 1990.

Staub, Jack. *75 Exceptional Herbs for Your Garden*. Layton, UT: Gibb Smith, 2008.

Stewart, R. J. *Celtic Myths, Celtic Legends.* London: Blandford (Cassell), 1996.

Storr, Anthony, ed. *The Essential Jung.* New York: Barnes & Noble Books, 1983.

Tallant, Robert. *Voodoo in New Orleans.* New Orleans: Pelican Publishing, 1983.

Tenzin-Dolma, Lisa. *Natural Mandalas.* London: Duncan Baird Publishers, 2006.

Teish, Luisah. *Jambalaya: The Natural Woman's Book of Personal Charms and Practical Rituals.* San Francisco: Harper, 1985.

"Traiteurs." Research Project No. 91, Folklore Collection Archives, University of Southwestern Louisiana, 1968.

"Tree and Plant Worship." www.sacred-texts.com/neu/celt/rac/rac16.htm (accessed December 2008).

"Tree Quotations." http://www.savatree.com/tree-quotes.html. (accessed March 2009).

"Trees." http://www.gardendigest.com/trees.htm (accessed March 2009).

"Unity in Diversity." http://farrid.20m.com/un.html (access date unknown).

Vega, Phyllis. *Celtic Astrology: How the Mystical Power of the Druid Tree Signs Can Transform Your Life.* Franklin Lakes, NJ: New Page Books, 2002.

"Voudooism—African Fetich Worship Among The Memphis Negroes." *The Memphis Appeal*, circa 1865–1867, cited by P. B.

Randolph, 1870. http://www.southern-spirits.com/avery-conjure.html (accessed January 2009).

Waring, Philippa. *A Dictionary of Omens and Superstitions*. London: Souvenir Press, 1978.

Weiss, Gaea, and Shandor Weiss. *Growing and Using Healing Herbs*. Emmaus, PA: Rodale, 1985.

Whitcomb, Bill. *The Magician's Companion: A Practical & Encyclopedic Guide to Magical & Religious Symbolism*. St. Paul, MN: Llewellyn, 2004.

"Wisdom of Trees in the Celtic Landscape." http://merganser.math.gvsu.edu/myth/trees.html. (accessed December 2008).

Worth, Valerie. *Crone's Book of Charms & Spells*. Woodbury, MN: Llewellyn, 2007.

Yronwode, Catherine. "Herb Magic." http://herb-magic.com. (accessed November 2008–January 2009).

———. *Hoodoo Herb and Root Magic: A Materia Magica of African-American Conjure*. Forestville, CA: Lucky Mojo Curio Company, 2002.